Flesh & Blood Volume 2
edited by Harvey Fenton

published by
FAB Press Ltd.
2 Farleigh
Ramsden Road
Godalming
Surrey
GU7 1QE
England, U.K.

www.fabpress.com

illustrations
front cover: Yutte Stensgaard's iconic appearance in **Lust for a Vampire**.
back cover: Promo image from the American theatrical poster for **Evil Dead II**.
side bar images, top to bottom: **Sweet Movie; Killer's Moon; The Vampire Lovers; RoboCop; The Decameron; Blood and Roses; The Evil Dead**.
frontispiece: Kirsten Betts in a scene from **The Vampire Lovers**.
title page (opposite): Detail from German theatrical poster for **Twins of Evil**.

acknowledgements
Alan Birkinshaw, James Blackford, Grete Kotryna Domarkaite, Stuart Gordon, Dick Klemensen, John Landis, Sam McKinlay, Tristan Thompson, Paul Verhoeven, Norman J. Warren, Nigel Wingrove, Geoffrey Wright.

acknowledgements are also due to the following organisations
Academy Entertainment, American Continental Films, British Film Institute, Brussels International Festival of Fantasy Film, Capitol International, CIC, Cineriz, The Cult Film Archive, EMI, Empire Pictures, Film & Entertainment VIP Medienfonds 4, Flipside, Fono Roma, Hammer Films, Kino Video, MGM, Palace Pictures, Paramount, Re-Animator Productions Inc, Redemption Films, Riverside Studios Hammersmith, Rob Houwer's Filmcompagnie, Sony Pictures, 20th Century Fox, Universal, Warner Bros, Wingnut Films, and anyone else who may have been inadvertently forgotten. Any omissions will be corrected in future editions.

Hardback limited edition:
ISBN 978-1-903254-66-0

Paperback:
ISBN 978-1-903254-67-7

A CIP catalogue record for this book is available from the British Library

First published September 2011

FLESH & BLOOD

VOLUME 2

**edited by
Harvey Fenton**

A
FAB
PRESS
PUBLICATION

editorial

It's been a long time coming, but it is with great pleasure that I invite you to peruse, and hopefully enjoy, this "resurrection edition" of *Flesh And Blood*, the cult movie journal that gave birth to FAB Press itself, way back in 1993.

Flesh And Blood Issue 1 was handed out to strangers queueing, on a cold February day, to get in to an all-night horror event at the Scala cinema in Kings Cross, London. The modest 20-page photocopied fanzine was a labour of love I had put together over the preceding couple of months; my attempt to give something back to the small but vibrant horror film fan scene that had sprung up in reaction to the UK's heavy-handed censorship of video tapes in the 1980s, and had gone on to thrive as the 1990s dawned and the power of the BBFC held sway. On a purely personal level it was inconceivable at the time that I would be here, a full 18 years later, typing this editorial, but in retrospect what is of more wide-reaching interest is to consider how, in some ways the whole cult movie fan scene is so very different nowadays, but also how much of it has remained remarkably familiar.

The sheer accessibility of cult movies is the most striking change of all; whereas in 1993 we had to either wait for cinematic temples such as the Scala to put those elusive classics up on the silver screen, or resort to third-generation VHS copies traded like drugs via a semi-criminal underground network, now it's all out there, digitally remastered. There's literally nothing a curious film fan cannot see these days without a little (minuscule, actually) degree of patience. If you did not experience those heady yet frustrating days you quite frankly have no idea at all how much of a buzz it was to finally see a long-lost wish-list inhabitant such as **Last House on Dead End Street**, or any number of Jess Franco obscurities, come to think of it...

Technology has changed everything... *FAB 1* was put together by a combination of an Amiga 500, scissors, glue, and a photocopier. E-mail was pretty much confined to the military and big business at that time, movies fanzines were traded by mail and paid for by Postal Orders and cheques... but the movies themselves... well, let's put it this way: **The Evil Dead**, **Suspiria** and **The Thing** still mean *precisely* the same thing to cult movie fans everywhere.

Some things don't so much change as move in cycles however, one example being the BBFC, who for much of the past decade had given the impression of listening to the voice of reason, but have sadly reverted to type lately, disgracing themselves with patronising decisions concerning the likes of **A Serbian Film** and **Human Centipede II**. As with the original 'video nasties', these films have thus been ushered – by their suppressors – to the front of every cult movie fan's 'must-see' list. So there you go; some things just don't change, really. Actually, it's slightly comforting, in a perverse kind of way...

So, with FAB Press now an 'adult' entity, having notched up 18 dramatic, unpredictable years, I can only guess at the adventures awaiting the next generation of cult movie fans, a further 18 years from now...

Harvey Fenton
August 2011

Editor Design Layout
Harvey Fenton

Indexing
Francis Brewster

Contributing Writers

Carl T. Ford
Kier-La Janisse
Xavier Mendik
Rocket Mortenson
Jamie Russell
Jonathan Sothcott
Marcus Stiglegger
Robert G. Weiner

Please send correspondence to the editorial address:

**Harvey Fenton / FAB Press
2 Farleigh, Ramsden Road
Godalming, Surrey
GU7 1QE
England, U.K.**

E-mail us:
harvey@fabpress.com

Visit our website:
www.fabpress.com

Contents

7

The Female of the Species
Fantale's Karnstein Trilogy
Jonathan Sothcott

19

An American Filmmaker in London
An Interview with John Landis
Jamie Russell

27

Sugar and Spice and All Things Nice
Sweet Movie and the Films of Dusan Makavejev
Carl T. Ford

35

The Killing Moon
An Interview with Alan Birkinshaw
Xavier Mendik

41

Boccaccio's Bastards
The Decameron from Pop to Porn
Kier-La Janisse

57

Adrenaline Vision
A Discussion with Australian Filmmaker Geoffrey Wright
Marcus Stiglegger

67

Prince of Exploitation
The Films of Dwain Esper
Robert G. Weiner

73

The (Un)Hollow Man
Paul Verhoeven Discusses the Politics of Pulp
Xavier Mendik

81

The Gore the Merrier
Slapstick, "Splatstick" and Body Horror
Jamie Russell

89

Blood and Roses
Roger Vadim's Erotic Vampire Classic Reassessed
Rocket Mortenson

The Female of the Species

Fantale's Karnstein Trilogy

Jonathan Sothcott

Joseph Sheridan Le Fanu's vampire novella *Carmilla* first appeared in serialisation form in the London magazine, *The Dark Blue*, in 1871 – a full quarter of a century before Bram Stoker unleashed *Dracula* on the unexpecting Victorian populace. Telling of a female vampire, Carmilla Karnstein, who preyed on lovely young girls rather than men, the story was a minor sensation that was eclipsed by Stoker's classic in due course and largely forgotten.

Despite predating Stoker's tale on the printed page, it took much longer for *Carmilla* to be translated to the silver screen, in the form of Carl Dreyer's **Vampyr** (1932). Though bearing only a passing resemblance to its source, the film's expressionistic style – it had more in common with **The Cabinet of Dr. Caligari** than **Dracula** – found favour with the critics. The Karnsteins then lay dormant on screen until 1960, when Roger Vadim retold the tale as **Blood and Roses**. Romanticised, even ethereal, it was far from a straightforward vampire film and is now barely remembered as a footnote in horror cinema *[Vadim's film is re-appraised in these very pages, as the final article in this volume of Flesh & Blood – Ed.]* It was a 1964 Spanish film, released under a myriad of different titles, but perhaps best known as **Crypt of Horror**, which first capitalised on the genuine sexual frissons in the story and contemporised this angle with fashionable horror by offering Christopher Lee as Count Karnstein. Despite such pleasing elements, it replaced the narrative's vampiric catalyst with a reincarnated witch, relegating it to the also-rans and leaving the way open for a definitive adaptation.

Independent producer Harry Fine was first taken with the idea of attempting such a version in early October 1969, whilst glancing through the *Dublin Gate Theatre Book*, in which he came across some stills from a play the Earl of Longford had adapted from *Carmilla* in the early thirties. Fine approached another producer, Michael Style, and a screenwriter, Tudor Gates, to join him in this proposed venture. Fine and Style had both worked for Tony Tenser before (Fine had produced 1965's **The Pleasure Girls** while, perhaps more relevantly, Style had produced the lesbian drama **Monique** for Tigon in 1969), and they first collaborated on a film in 1968, in the shape of the Joan Collins/Suzanna Leigh spy nonsense **Subterfuge**. Tudor Gates

had been Harry Fine's assistant theatre manager in the mid fifties and had gone on to write several episodes of Fine-produced TV shows as well as contributing to the **Barbarella** screenplay. Working under the banner of Fantale Films (a company Fine had set up for his own uses a couple of years previously), the triumvirate thrashed out a basic plot structure, from which Gates produced a five page story outline to drum up backing. As Gates himself recalls, "Hammer were the only people [in Britain] making films at the time, so they were the obvious choice." Hammer chief James Carreras, greatly taken by the clear lesbian direction of the treatment, was decidedly eager to film it – and moreso because it was the first script he had received which, anticipating the raising of the age of admission to films bearing the 'X' certificate from 16 to 18, had beefed up its racy content accordingly.

With Warner Bros–Seven Arts now out of the picture as Hammer's regular financier, Carreras approached Samuel Z. Arkoff and James H. Nicholson of AIP (perhaps mindful of the fact that they had recently funded Amicus's **Scream and Scream Again**) and in typical fashion sold the idea to them over a swanky meal. On 25 November 1969, Fantale finalised a deal to produce the film, now titled **The Vampire Lovers**, on Hammer's behalf, which would entitle them to 25% of Hammer's profits from sales of the picture. Prior to this deal, Hammer had not been in a situation whereby they were literally sub-contracting another company to make a horror film for them, but then they had never before been without a major American backer.

above: Nightmarish cemetery imagery from **The Vampire Lovers**.
opposite: A contact sheet showing Ingrid Pitt in her prime on **The Vampire Lovers**.

Carreras agreed that Hammer would guarantee any over-budget expenses. Two weeks later, AIP injected the necessary $400,000 (c. £170,000) into the project in a deal which would entitle them to full distribution rights in America. The modest budget was indicative of Hammer's downward spiral after the end of the Seven Arts deal. In comparison, earlier in the year, even the psycho-thriller **Crescendo**, a minor production for Hammer bankrolled by the deal, had cost £299,000.

Even before AIP officially signed on, casting the film had proved convoluted. Theatrical agent John Redway put forward Shirley Eaton for the pivotal role of Carmilla. As a result of her appearances in **Doctor in the House** (1954), three of the first 'Carry On's and some half a dozen other popular comedies, Eaton was a popular iconographic sex symbol of naïve post-war Britain. She gained international recognition for her gold-coated role in **Goldfinger** (1964); following this she graced the cover of *Life* magazine, but aside from an excellent turn in **Ten Little Indians** (1965) the Bond outing did little to enhance her career, and something of a lull ensued. During the last few years of the sixties she appeared in the Sax Rohmer Fu Manchu companion pieces **The Million Eyes of Sumuru** (1967) and its 1968 sequel **Rio 70** (a number of her scenes from which were then cheekily stitched into the following year's **The Blood of Fu Manchu**, billing her as a 'special guest star') before she took a break to start a family. When I mentioned it to her, Eaton was completely unaware that she had been put forward for the role, but considered it one she wouldn't have cared to play anyway because of the nudity required. Why she was ultimately knocked back remains something of a mystery: James Carreras wrote to Harry Fine suggesting that at "about 32" she was too old for the part. In reality it is far more likely they didn't want to overspend on the female lead and Eaton would have been more expensive than their usual dolly birds.

Instead, the role went to Polish émigré Ingrid Pitt, then-girlfriend of George Pinches, the Rank circuit booking manager. Carreras had met her at the **Alfred the Great** (1969) première party, and noted to Harry Fine that she "looked great" in her sassy supporting role in **Where Eagles Dare** (1968). Pitt appeared at a Fantale audition one morning, and though impressed by her reading, Tudor Gates noted that, "We [Fantale] were only endorsing someone else's decision." Carreras was later forced to defend this decision to the Ministry of Labour, who were curious as to why no British actress could be found for the role.

Tudor Gates's 120-page screenplay, dated 15 December 1969, incorporates several interesting sequences absent from the finished film. Foremost

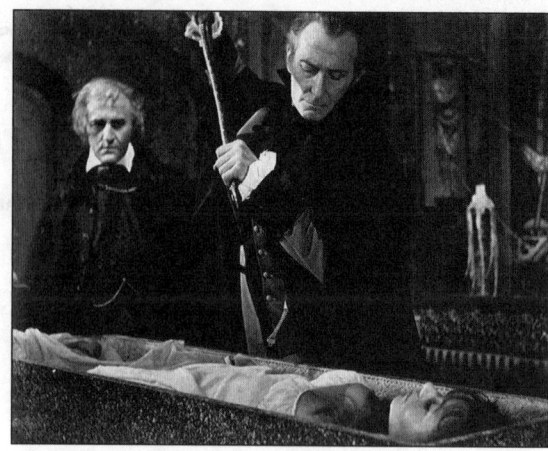

above: Peter Cushing prepares to stake Ingrid Pitt in **The Vampire Lovers**.
opposite: Polish émigré Pitt was awarded the role of Carmilla by James Carreras.

amongst these was a scene that was to have taken place once Carmilla was safely ensconced within the bosom of the Morton family. A mute, medieval-type Jester (replete with garish costume and silly hat) appears at the house to entertain Emma, who calls Carmilla out to watch. The Jester then sells Emma a magic charm to ward off vampires. This understandably angers Carmilla, who attacks him, for she knows that he senses her to be a vampire. Sent packing by Carmilla and the Governess, his gestured warnings go unheeded by Emma. This scene was dropped late in the day as Aubrey Morris (later seen as the inn keeper in **The Wicker Man**) was cast in the role but never made it to set.

Hammer nominated the dependable Roy Ward Baker to direct, a proposition deemed acceptable by the Fantale team. Hammer's business affairs hotshot Brian Lawrence had to decline Baker's request to also produce, palming him off with the possibility of producing **Scars of Dracula** instead (in the end Baker never produced a film for Hammer). Perhaps weary of his interference during the filming of Tigon's **The Haunted House of Horror** (1969), Harry Fine obtained a specific undertaking from James Carreras and AIP that 'Deke' Heyward would not meddle in the production, subject to general approval of the script and the casting of the leads. This latter task caused AIP some concern, and they intimated that they would feel more "secure" with a "typical Hammer cast". Presumably as a result of this, Peter Cushing was offered a cameo early in the new year. Unsurprisingly, Christopher Lee passed on Hammer's offer of the Man in Black/Count Karnstein part. Both Cushing and Pitt were introduced to the press at a glitzy reception at The Savoy on Tuesday, 13 January 1970.

Filming commenced six days later, on Monday, 19 January amid an ongoing correspondence between Hammer and a concerned BBFC. Censor John Trevelyan was so worried by the script's uncompromising blend of blood-letting and lesbianism that he sent a confidential letter to (by then 'Sir') James Carreras, asking him to use his "personal influence" to keep Fine and Style in check. The film's nude scenes were shot on a closed set to protect the stars' modesty, which lead to a slightly dejected Fine and Style bumping into Pitt in an Elstree corridor just after she'd filmed her bath scene. Ever game, Pitt dropped her robe and gave them an eyeful of what they'd missed, adding a little spring to their steps.

The distinguished supporting cast, one of the film's chief assets, included a number of performers who had worked for Hammer previously, amongst them: Dawn Addams, who had starred in **The Two Faces of Dr. Jekyll** (1960); Kate O'Mara, who made her big screen debut in **Captain Clegg** (1962); lovely Kirsten Betts, previously seen in **Crescendo**; and Madeline Smith, who had featured very briefly in a bordello scene in the previous year's **Taste the Blood of Dracula**. The male cast included: George Cole (who had appeared in one

this page: Ingrid Pitt was entirely comfortable with the nudity that was a requisite part of her role in **The Vampire Lovers**.

of Hammer's early comedies); Ferdy Mayne (who all but stole every scene in Roman Polanski's magnificent 1967 vampire spoof **Dance of the Vampires**); and Jon Finch (in his film debut), who really made his mark in 1971, when he appeared in both Polanski's **Macbeth** and the Hitchcock thriller **Frenzy**.

Principal photography wrapped on 4 March 1970 (slightly under budget at just £165, 227) and despite claiming "disinterest" in the film's lesbian angle, Roy Ward Baker considered himself pleased with the end result – "A risky subject in which I avoided vulgarity and surprised some people", as he told me. By the time the film was shown to the trade at Metro House on 3 September, its sequel, **Lust for a Vampire**, was already in the can.

Following a première at the New Victoria on 4 October, the film went on general release on the ABC circuit, double-billed with a trashy biker programmer, **Angels from Hell** (1970), where the Hammer board considered its performance "normal". Bored critics echoed this view – "Terribly cobbled-up in script and direction", offered *The Times*, while in America, John L. Wasserman of *The San Francisco Chronicle* opted for a more intricate attack on the film: "Peter Cushing, who struggles along in this sort of thing regularly, co-stars with a bevy of beauties, none of whom will ever be heard from again… The director, whoever he may be, manages to present their principal assets with enthusiasm and regularity." Word of mouth obviously helped, however, as it soon broke a couple of attendance records, leading the board to later revise their appraisal of its returns to "excellent". By 9 December, the double bill had taken £33, 269 in North London and £25, 628 in South London. On the same date, the Hammer board learned that AIP reported "very good figures" in the States, and they confidently expected the picture to make over $1,000,000. Hammer's first horror film of the seventies would also prove to be by far their most successful in America that decade.

The fundamental flaw with the formidable reputation of **The Vampire Lovers** is that it isn't half as innovative as its admirers make out. The visually pleasing female cast are for the most part wasted in the roles of simpering, mentally anaemic ninnies, but even the older, more experienced Kate O'Mara and Dawn Addams have almost nothing to do but pout and scowl. The trio of ageing heroes – Cushing, Wilmer and Cole – do little but assume grim expressions and mumble amongst themselves about how best to destroy vampires. Tudor Gates's script, though forcefully thrusting the female vampire to the fore, and allowing for some remarkable set piece killings, is, at times, a little *too* faithful to Le Fanu's staid, repetitive novella. That the script basically tells the same story twice (what happens to Pippa Steel happens almost exactly to Madeline

Smith) can be overlooked, as no pretence that Carmilla is anything other than a vampire is attempted. The rather coy nudity was a first for a domestic release of a Hammer horror, and while it certainly doesn't detract from the film, it adds little to it – actresses such as Valerie Gaunt and Isobel Black had previously proved to be sexier with clothes on than anyone in **The Vampire Lovers** is without them. Ingrid Pitt's wanton Carmilla is very different to the regal, commanding vampire Shirley Eaton might have been (ironically, Pitt was criticised by some reviewers as being too old for the part) – yet as the permissive society caught up with Hammer's Gothic romance, her animalistic sexual predator seems quite appropriate, and her performance stands out as one of the film's few points of lasting interest. Though plodding, **The Vampire Lovers** remains a fan favourite; primarily by virtue of Ingrid Pitt's dominant performance, and as a straightforward vampire film, spiced up with a few bare breasts, it is a thoroughly enjoyable and accessible piece of entertainment.

above: Hammer's customary gentleman hero, Peter Cushing, seen here with young starlet Pippa Steel in **The Vampire Lovers**.

The Fantale team began discussing ideas for a sequel to **The Vampire Lovers** as soon as they had a deal with Hammer to finance it. Sir James Carreras was optimistic enough about the success of **The Vampire Lovers** to initiate the first script conference for this sequel, provisionally titled 'To Love a Vampire', on 21 January 1970 – only two days after Carmilla Karnstein's first Hammer outing had commenced filming.

The idea of an aristocratic vampire of undecided sexuality let loose in a girls' finishing school was nothing new; it had already been done by Hammer as far back as 1960, in the form of the infinitely superior **The Brides of Dracula**, but Gates updated the formula (borrowing the basic structure from an earlier script of his, 'Cry Nightmare') with a robust injection of coy nudity and explicit gore.

Gates's screenplay, decidedly more character-driven than **The Vampire Lovers**, was little changed by the time the film was completed, with only one exposure (Janet) and one murder (Miss Simpson) removed in terms of narrative events.

Gates wrote the part of slimy occult student and history teacher Giles Barton specifically for Peter Cushing, then busy with his cameo in **The Vampire Lovers**. With Carreras confident that AIP would bankroll the project, Ingrid Pitt was expected to reprise her Carmilla role, while Hammer's original auteur, Terence Fisher, was busy preparing to direct what would have been his first non-Dracula vampire film since **The Brides of Dracula**. Looking back it is hard to imagine Cushing or Fisher attaching themselves to material as trashy as this, or anyone buying the idea of Ingrid Pitt as a young student, but fate was to take an unexpected turn.

On 25 February, Roy Skeggs suggested that shooting in May/June could make use of Hammer's Bray Studios facility. The company had kept the Thames-side studio mothballed since production ended on **The Mummy's Shroud** in 1966 (though

effects work on both **Moon Zero Two** and **When Dinosaurs Ruled the Earth** had been conducted there), as it hadn't been prudent to maintain a permanent staff. This meant that a new crew would have to have been hired; an impractical investment for just one film. Added to that was the fact that Skeggs was in the midst of negotiations to sell the property (a deal was eventually clinched in November 1970, when Hammer managed to offload the studio to Redspring Ltd.), which would undoubtedly have caused interruptions to the flow of filming. By Spring, however, use of Bray Studios was no longer an option. When AIP passed over the film in favour of developing their own horror subjects, James Carreras struck a deal with Bernard Delfont for EMI to handle the film's British and European release. As with all EMI-funded projects, the use of the company's Elstree studio became a condition of the deal.

Full time pre-production began in May (and continued throughout June), and was marred by a series of unforseeable near-catastrophes. Injured in a road traffic accident (his second in only a few years), Terence Fisher was forced to release the directorial reigns. Harry Fine initially toyed with the idea of filling in for Fisher himself but, as luck would have it, regular Hammer writer/producer Jimmy Sangster was in London working on post-production for **Horror of Frankenstein**, and he accepted Fine's offer to direct. Peter Cushing, whose wife Helen was seriously ill with what would develop into terminal emphysema, was also allowed to bow out, after appealing personally to Sir James Carreras.

With the withdrawal of AIP as backers, along went Ingrid Pitt's reprisal of her **Vampire Lovers** role. She was replaced by sexy Danish blonde Yutte Stensgaard.

With only a string of small roles in such films as **Zeta One** and **Doctor in Trouble** behind her, she lacked Pitt's Hollywood pedigree, and her faltering command of the English language ("Yes, it's quite good… it's very… it's a very good part. There is quite a lot of things happening", was her summation of her role in a contemporary profile) would eventually lead to her being comprehensively dubbed. However, her eminently photogenic figure and beguiling beauty were adequate compensations. Unfortunately, her performance lacked the depth and animalistic ferocity which Ingrid Pitt had brought to the role, and she elicits little empathy. Despite harbouring Academy Award designs (on her ambitions: "I think to become a very good actress and hope to get an Oscar sometime"), her film career was over by the mid-seventies and she moved to Oregon where she proceeded to enjoy a more succesful career selling radio air time.

Jimmy Sangster's new pal from **Horror of Frankenstein**, Ralph Bates, was drafted in to fill Cushing's shoes as Barton ("As favour to Jimmy & Peter", gentlemanly Bates explained) and elected to play the part as a pervy young academic. As such, aided by Gates's re-tailoring of the part to suit him, Bates gave what is certainly the film's best performance, relatively restrained in general, despite a smattering of enthusiastic of scenery-chewing. While directing **Horror of Frankenstein**, Sangster had been introduced to charismatic ex-BBC DJ Mike Raven, who was eager to get into horror films. Sangster said there was nothing for him in the film, and Raven presumed that he'd been given a polite brush off. He was thrilled silly then, when Sangster called him a few months later to audition for the part of Count Karnstein. Sadly Raven's genre debut is not all he'd hoped for, due to awful dubbing by Valentine Dyall, and incessant close-ups of Christopher Lee's eyes, lifted from **Dracula Has Risen from the Grave**. Raven enjoyed a short movie career, appearing in a few more cheesy horror films, before becoming a sculptor.

The rest of the cast were equally eclectic. One-time Elvisette Suzanna Leigh, who hadn't made a film since **Subterfuge** in 1968, was in dire financial straits at the time. Ringing dependable Sir James on the Friday before production commenced, she called in a favour to replace another actress already cast as Janet Playfair. Kirsten Betts (née Lindholm) returned from **The Vampire Lovers**, as did Harvey Hall and Pippa Steel. Judy Matheson, one of the busiest starlets of the period, appeared as one of Mircalla's topless schoolgirl 'victims'. Another of these young ladies was played by a former schoolteacher, Sue Longhurst (in real life pushing thirty), appearing in her first British film. Throughout the rest of the decade, Longhurst was awarded leading roles

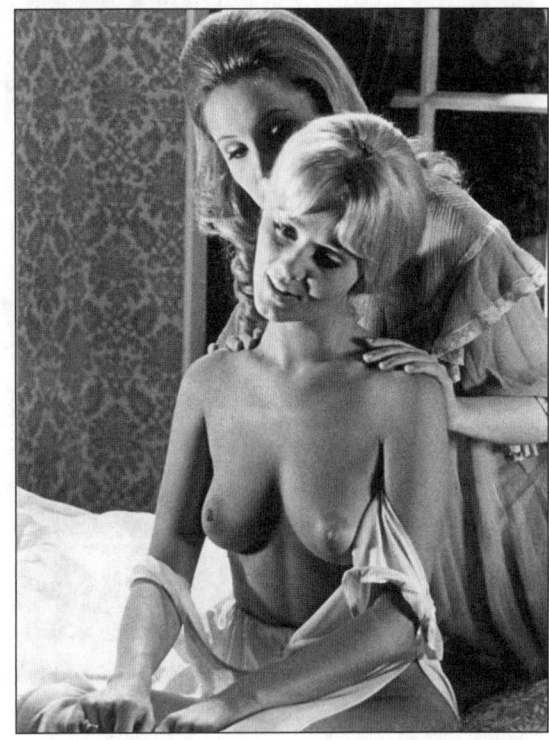

this page and opposite:
The second of the Hammer trilogy produced by Fantale, **Lust for a Vampire**, stayed faithful to the fangs-and-boobs template laid down by its predecessor. Glamour was provided by Yutte Stensgaard, whilst former DJ Mike Raven exploited his reputed interest in the occult, as he was awarded the role of Count Karnstein (*below*).

in a seemingly endless run of sex comedies, including **Confessions of a Window Cleaner**, **Can You Keep It Up for a Week?** and **Keep It Up Downstairs**.

Principal photography began on 6 July, at Elstree and also a nearby country house, which was used for exterior shots of the school. The shoot was a relatively straightforward one, though Sangster didn't get on at all well with new boys Fine and Style, and filming wrapped on 18 August. Once the film was in the can, its most controversial element raised its head. Sir James had seen a rough cut, still titled 'To Love a Vampire', by 9 September and noted that he was "quite pleased" with it. It has been suggested that Harry Fine had been quite taken with the song in **Butch Cassidy and the Sundance Kid**, and felt that a musical number would be equally successful in **Lust for a Vampire**. Composer Harry Robertson, in collaboration with independent producer (and Robertson's then-manager) Frank Godwin, wrote a pleasant enough little ditty, 'Strange Love', and selected EMI contract artiste 'Tracy' to sing it. Hammer's long-time musical supervisor Philip Martell was having none of this, and took his complaint directly to Sir James. Carreras offered a solution: if it cost him anything, it was out, if it could be included in the budget, it remained. Fine kept it within his budget, and recorded the music on the 23rd and 24th of September and the song on the 28th. Mixing took place the following week. Tracy's reasonably melodious, though decidedly inappropriate, strains were later released as

a single on EMI's Columbia label. Predictably, the disc is now a much sought-after collector's item.

Bernard Delfont, feeling that 'To Love a Vampire' was too arty a title, insisted upon the change to the more familiar **Lust for a Vampire** late in post-production. When the film was submitted to the BBFC, it was granted an 'X' certificate, on the condition that Hammer deleted the scene in Reel 5 where Stensgaard lay on a naked girl – "this whole scene must be removed". The film was shown to the trade on 8 December, at Metro House.

With **The Vampire Lovers** making *Kine Weekly's* 'Top Moneymakers' list of 1970, **Lust for a Vampire** was released in Britain on 17 January 1971. "Fairly routine vampire stuff", declared *Kine Weekly*; "Tepid horror pic, more humorous than frightening", agreed *Variety*. Neither a fanfare of publicity nor a tie-in paperback by William Hughes could save it. Released on a double bill with **The Losers**, it failed to ignite the box office in the way its prequel had. The reason for this is uncertain – perhaps due to its lack of a 'name' star, perhaps because **The Vampire Lovers** was still on release in the provinces. What became clear was that eleven years on from **Brides of Dracula**, the words 'Hammer' and 'Vampire' no longer guaranteed queues at the domestic box office. The film fared even worse Stateside: sold to cheapjack outfit Continental, it was barely released, despite needing to be cut for the requisite 'R' certificate.

Despite a well-intentioned script (perhaps the most thoughtful and romantic of Gates's Karnstein Trilogy) and acceptable performances, the film remains one of Hammer's least popular offerings. The theme song, lack of Cushing and Fisher, and the obvious cost cutting (even the burning castle is lifted from the end of **Scars of Dracula**) are factors most often cited for the film's unpopularity. That now notorious song, innocuous enough in itself, can be enjoyed today as an amusing diversion. The lack of Hammer's old guard is perhaps best viewed as a lucky escape (it's hard to imagine Fisher being in synch with the material and Cushing would presumably have imposed his 'Dr. Who' characterisation on the part of Barton), but there is no excuse for the film's inherent cheapness. As such, it misses the mark in many ways – hindsight particularly reveals it to be less innovative than its prequel, and also patently inferior to its splendid sequel. While this can be chalked up to the head-on collision of Hammer's old (Sangster) and new (Fantale) creative forces, there remains little excuse; the film's enigmatic cult status puts it squarely in the 'so bad it's good' category.

In summary, **Lust for a Vampire** is guilty of all charges – it is cheap, it is tacky, it is silly – but for some reason it is fondly remembered for being so, and it has become established as an fun addition to the Hammer Horror cycle.

For the third instalment in Hammer and Fantale's on-going chronicle of the Karnstein family, the original concept came from James Carreras, who was clearly enjoying the new decade's embracing of increasingly permissive cinema, and decreed that a film with sexy (and preferably topless) twin vampires was what was needed. Initially, the project was touted as 'The Gemini Twins', while Fantale busied itself with a separate story outline entitled 'Village of Vampires'. With one eye on the box office, Carreras decided that the market was already glutted with vampire exploitation films and that the two ideas should be stitched into one screenplay, which Tudor Gates dutifully wrote and submitted as **Twins of Evil**. The conflicting storylines were successfully amalgamated, but at the expense of continuity – the new script was set in the 18th Century European domain of Quaker-like witchfinders, ruled by a fearsome overlord referred to only as 'The Emperor'. Carmilla Karnstein, the narrative link of the first two films made only a guest appearance in Gates's latest tale; the whole plot took on darker tones, exploring class war and religion, and asked the audience to decide whether it was the vampires or their puritanical opposition who were the true villains of the piece.

As had been their intention with 'Village of the Vampires', Rank agreed to finance the latest addition to the Karnstein saga, and Hammer signed a deal with Fantale on 5 January 1971. After their frayed relationship with Jimmy Sangster, Fine and Style were keen to have a fresh directorial approach, and gladly seconded Hammer's proposal – 29-year-old John Hough. Hough had gained a reputation as one of the sharpest directors on the British television scene in the late sixties, working to great acclaim on shows like **The Saint** and, to a greater extent, **The Avengers**, where he had served as a long standing second unit director, before assuming singular control of several of the latter episodes starring Linda Thorson. Hough had come to Hammer's attention via an abortive TV pilot he had directed in 1969: **Wolfshead: The Legend of Robin Hood**, in which they had an interest, and readily took the directorial reins. Hough was soon confronted with a most difficult bit of casting – that of the titular identical twins. Though actresses including Caroline Munro and Kate O'Mara were considered in the early stages, they were soon nixed when no suitable lookalikes could be found, and it was decided that trick photography would add a dimension of tackiness – as well as extra cost! Hough eventually screen tested three pairs of twins (nine other pairs had been rejected by this time): **Virgin Witch**'s Ann and Vicki Michelle; a popular blonde modelling duo known as the Baker Twins; and Maltese-born Mary and Madeleine Collinson, who had gained infamy as *Playboy*'s first twin playmates, appearing in the October 1970 issue. Though they lacked extensive film experience, they had appeared in several sex comedies and captured the roles by virtue of their dark good looks, as John Hough recalled: "They had a kind of mysterious, exotic quality that none of the others possessed."

this page: The most overtly violent film of the trilogy, **Twins of Evil** starred genuine siblings Mary and Madeleine Collinson (*top*).

Less than two months after the death of his beloved wife, Peter Cushing agreed to take the role of Gustave Weil, the puritanical head of 'The Brotherhood' – a role that Tudor Gates had written especially for him, in an attempt to help him break away from his usual performances. As he had lost a considerable amount of weight during Helen's illness, Cushing's subsequent appearance was startlingly gaunt and emaciated, adding stark realism to what would be one of the grimmest parts he ever played.

Principal photography began at Pinewood Studios on 22 March 1971. The cast featured a number of performers of whom Hammer expected 'big things' – particularly the darkly handsome Damien Thomas who was, at one time, suggested as a potential Dracula when Christopher Lee jumped ship, and the gorgeous Katya Wyeth – the screen's most striking Carmilla – who had played a bit role in Hammer's **Hands of the Ripper** and would go on to star in the underrated **Straight On Till Morning** later in the year. Kirsten Lindholm once again appeared, making her the only actress to feature in the whole Karnstein triumvirate, while amongst the male cast a similar honour befell Harvey Hall.

Mary and Madeleine Collinson were the film's main point of interest both on and off set. Both spent time with a voice coach in order to perfect their English diction, and contrary to some reports, were not revoiced in the finished film. In fact, it was their different vocal tones that enabled the crew to differentiate between them, as John Hough later explained. Despite a veritable mountain of press hand-outs asking 'Witch is Which?', Damien Thomas found out soon enough during shooting, when he broke one of his custom-made fangs on Madeleine's neck!

The filming was completed on 30 April, at a final cost of £205,067 – particularly impressive as the film is, arguably, Hammer's most lavish of the decade. A scene was lost during editing amid fears that the BBFC would clamp down hard on the liberal mix of blood and bosoms, and Karnstein's stripping of Frieda in her prison cell was refilmed so as to be witnessed as shadows on a wall. Ultimately, the British censor passed

this page and opposite: Featuring a graphic fiery execution, beheading, nudity and vampiric breast-biting, **Twins of Evil** proved to be a suitable double-bill partner for the similarly risqué horror film **Hands of the Ripper**, as Hammer settled comfortably into the X-rated 1970s.

the submitted print uncut. Following a trade show on 24 September, the film earned a roster of good reviews, the likes of which no Hammer film had garnered since **The Devil Rides Out**. *Cinema & TV Today* lead the way with their praise: "Dick Bush's excellent photography… provides the gloss that is the film's most impressive quality", while even the *Monthly Film Bulletin* was forced to admit that the film was, "easily the best of Hammer's vampire films in some time." In the wake of this positive press reaction came a glitzy premiere attended by the Collinson Twins, Peter Cushing and Katya Wyeth, along with several of those involved in the making of the film's co-feature **Hands of the Ripper**. The double bill was released in early October, taking an impressive £4,379 in its first week at the New Victoria, and continuing to do well throughout the provinces. The Collinsons gave the film additional publicity by touring various regional theatres.

In America, the film had been sold to CIC, who had retitled it **Twins of Dracula**. This misleading change of title was insufficient to save Hammer's most violent film from the scissors of the American censors, who snipped 5 minutes and 36 seconds before passing the film with the requisite 'R' certificate. CIC kept their new title for the film's Australian release. When the film was sold to American television, additional scenes, directed by Irving Moore, were inserted to increase the film's running time and cover the holes left by the censors.

Rightly regarded as the best of the Karnstein Trilogy, **Twins of Evil** is a stylish, superior horror film, which blends perfectly the themes which distinguished the first (evil aristocrat in castle on hill, unknown middle-European setting, Peter Cushing) and second (lesbianism, nudity, decapitations, nudity, stirring music, more nudity) waves of successful Hammer Horror films. The only time it wavers and plummets from the sublime to the camp is the scene in which Count Karnstein's mute servant acts out a brief game of charades of the villagers running at

the castle, armed with stakes, crosses and axes, as Karnstein readily plays along, his rage building to a crescendo. This 'Carry On'-like scene considerably lowers the tone of the last reel – but this minor flaw is but a little quibble given the film's overall quality. The performances throughout are superb, with Peter

above: Damien Thomas features in this haunting composite shot from **Twins of Evil**.

Cushing on outstanding form in a beautifully detailed study of authoritarian pomposity. Though she has only one scene, Katya Wyeth makes an impression as the sexiest of the Carmillas and the collection of lovely supporting actresses – Maggie Wright, Isobel Black, Luan Peters, Judy Matheson and Kirsten Lindholm amongst them – is as fine a selection of British screen crumpet as any contemporary film offers. The talent behind the camera is equally impressive, with John Hough pulling out all the stops to deliver an action-packed romp, one of the very best of Hammer's later offerings. Special mention must also be made of Harry Robertson's exceptional, pounding score – the finest

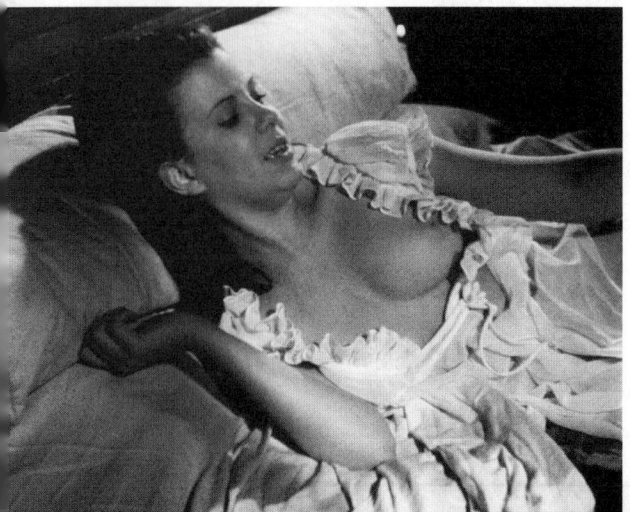

theme for a Hammer Gothic in the seventies. The music was released, as a rock 'n' roll mix, in late 1971, to little fanfare and has, thankfully, since slipped from sight.

With **Twins of Evil** deemed a success, a fourth installment in Hammer's latest franchise was considered a goer, and Tudor Gates busied himself with a new story outline, suggestively titled 'Vampire Virgins'. Gates told me that he and his partners genuinely thought they'd go on making these vampire films for Hammer forever. It was not to be. Though the film was never formally optioned by Hammer, a fourteen-page story treatment was produced, a copy of which was sent to Peter Cushing, who agreed to play one of the Karnsteins. Alternatively known as 'Vampire Hunters', the story deals with a pair of wandering vampire bounty killers, Kurt and Johann, who try to blackmail some villagers who won't pay up for services rendered. All fall foul of Count Karnstein, who vampirises a bevy of village girls, before succumbing to a wooden stake. Featuring such ambitious notions as teleportation and an orgy in a hay field, the film was dropped when Michael Carreras took over Hammer, particularly as it bore a striking similarity to Brian Clemens's **Captain Kronos: Vampire Hunter**, which the company had already optioned by that time.

Since then, Fantale's Karnstein clan have remained dormant, though other producers have subsequently attempted to remake Le Fanu's novel; most notable was the European film **The Blood Spattered Bride** starring Alexandra Bastedo, but even this fell well short of rivalling the Hammer/Fantale trio. The films have influenced public perception of the vampire too, and their influence on the vampire film was immediate – as early as 1971, Robert Quarry gleefully watched **The Vampire Lovers** on television in **The Return of Count Yorga**, while films such as **The Hunger**, **Daughters of Darkness**, **The Velvet Vampire**, **Vampyres** and even **Vamp** owe much to Tudor Gates's characters and stories. Though perhaps the weakest of the three, **The Vampire Lovers** marked a genuine watershed for the cinematic juxtaposition of sex and horror and launched Ingrid Pitt on the road to iconoclasm as the ultimate screen vamp. **Lust for a Vampire**, a victim of circumstance, is notable for Tudor Gates's remarkable prescience in anticipating the trend for romantic, female-driven vampire films. **Twins of Evil**, far and away the most effective of the trilogy, has lost little of its impact today, and offers a glimpse of the direction in which Fantale might have taken Hammer, had their relationship lasted longer. As a creative body of work, The Karnstein Trilogy stands as a fine achievement, and one which has undeniably left its mark on the cinema of the fantastic.

ↄ⊃

Jonathan Sothcott's company *Black and Blue Films* has been producing 21st Century horror pictures in the UK.

An American Filmmaker in London

An Interview with John Landis

Jamie Russell

In May 2007, John Landis was in the UK as a special guest of honour at the Sci-Fi London Film Festival. A magazine sent me down to the Apollo Cinema at Piccadilly Circus to interview him for a retrospective feature on his career. What was supposed to be a 20-minute interview getting bite-sized quotes on his filmography for a throwaway feature turned into an epic two-day marathon.

It was probably one of the most enjoyable interviews I've ever done, although I can honestly say that on a query/time ratio I've never asked so few questions during such a long interview. Landis is a brilliant person to approach with a tape recorder: a fantastic raconteur and a passionate cinephile. But his expansive style isn't exactly suited to a 20-minute slot with nervous PRs pacing outside the door!

We were already running behind when director Stuart Gordon – at the festival with his movie **Edmond** – walked into the interview and dragged us even further off topic. What follows is pieced together from about two hours of interviews spread over two days….

*Tell me about one of your earliest films, **The Kentucky Fried Movie**. It has a real edge to it, doesn't it?*

A lot of films I made were fairly radical at the time. **Kentucky Fried Movie** was a very outrageous movie and it came out at a time when no one had done stuff like that before. Now it's kind of a standard genre. These days they make parody movies that don't exist for any reason other than the jokes. **Kentucky Fried Movie** actually got very mixed reviews but there were people who enjoyed it. It was the mid-'70s, there was a lot of interesting comedy coming out around the world. It was fun. It's certainly silly.

I haven't seen that movie for at least five or six years, but there are things in it I still like. I really enjoyed the Bruce Lee parody [the segment known as "A Fistful of Yen"]. I think it really looks good. I mean, we had no money. **Kentucky Fried Movie** was made for half a million dollars and shot in twenty days. Evan Kim, the young guy who plays the Bruce Lee part, was quite a find. Not many people that adept at martial arts are also funny.

I actually knew Bruce Lee. I was working in the mailroom at Fox when they used to do **The Green Hornet**. I used to watch Bruce working out. He had a punching bag suspended 12 feet off the ground. Bruce was a tiny little guy and he would kick it, but not just kick it but fly in the air and kick it three times and land like a cat. It was so fast it was bizarre. You know Michael Jordan? They called him Air Jordan because he would literally fly. That's what Bruce did. It was amazing. A lot of what those martial arts guys would do was so fast it was impossible to shoot. You had to shoot at high speed and then it would just look fake.

We couldn't afford a real stunt person, so I was the guy in the gorilla suit. We called the gorilla Dino. I had a bunch of meetings with producer Dino De Laurentiis when I was about 25. He wanted to make a big monster movie and I asked my agent, "Does he mean make monster like Godzilla or make monster like big budget?" I met him and what he actually wanted was a monster movie disaster film. He wanted a disaster movie like **The Poseidon Adventure** but with a giant monster in it that would cause great destruction. So I suggested **King Kong**. We screened it for him with a bunch of Ray Harryhausen movies and **Godzilla**. Then I got hired on **The Spy Who Loved Me** and came over to England. While I was in London there was a big announcement that Dino De Laurentiis was going to remake **King Kong**. Carlo Rambaldi [the Italian SFX

above: Film director John Landis also takes the occasional acting role; here he is seen in the part of Dr. Levine in **Surviving Eden** (2004).

artist who worked on **Deep Red**, **Close Encounters of the Third Kind** and **E.T.: The Extra-Terrestrial**] convinced Dino that they could make a 68-foot robot gorilla. I thought that was absurd. I called Dino up and told him, "You're going to end up with a guy in a gorilla suit, because if you're not doing stop-motion photography – this was before CG – this won't work. And if you're going to end up with a guy in a gorilla suit you should speak to Rick Baker." To humour me, Dino met with Rick. Within a week Rick made a demo gorilla suit. He did it so fast. My wife Deborah and his then wife Elaine actually sewed the fur on it! And that was the gorilla suit we used in **Kentucky Fried Movie** and that's why we called him Dino.

*Another of your early comedies was **National Lampoon's Animal House**, which I'd describe as the mother of all teen comedies. Would you agree? Can you see the link from it to later movies like **American Pie**?*

Actually, **Animal House** is a direct descendant of **American Graffiti**, which had come out a year or two before. In terms of a certain kind of raucous comedy, though, yes – it's the mother of all teen comedies.

When I was hired to rewrite **Animal House** it was my first studio film. They offered the screenplay of **Animal House** to people like Mike Nichols and Dick Lester, who all threw it back in their face. They gave it to me and I thought it was one the funniest scripts I'd ever read but also very offensive. It was racist and sexist and anti-Semitic. I told them to make some changes. I was originally hired to supervise the screenplay rewrite. In the first draft everyone was a pig, you couldn't tell the difference between the Deltas and the Omegas. There weren't any good guys or bad guys.

Making it was a great experience. It was such a low-budget movie and such a small project for the studio that we were pretty much left alone. John [Belushi] became a huge star because of it. He was a celebrity from the television show **Saturday Night Live**, where he was kind of a cult star. His character in **Animal House** was written for him. But when I met him, I took away half his dialogue because he was such a great comedian he didn't need them. Clearly this character

Bluto is all about appetite. John and I talked about it quite a lot and we decided to turn him into Harpo Marx and the Cookie Monster rolled into one. He had to be sweet. He's completely destructive and voracious like the Cookie Monster but he had to be sweet like Harpo.

When it came out, it was a big giant hit. It was getting terrible reviews but now it's in the Library of Congress and considered a great American film. What happened? Nothing, it's the same movie it always was. **Animal House** gave me the power to make something as outrageous as **The Blues Brothers**. And that gave me the power to make **An American Werewolf in London**, which I wrote way back in 1969 but didn't make until 1981.

[Stuart Gordon walks in unexpectedly and sits down…]

SG: Don't believe a word this man says!
JL: Oh my God they will let anyone into this country! This is Stuart Gordon.
JR: I know who it is. Pleased to meet you, sir. I'm Jamie Russell.
JL: Are you interviewing Stuart?
JR: No, just you actually.
SG: I'm just going to sit here if that's OK.
JL: I want to quote Stuart. Stuart made a movie called **Re-Animator**. He's made a lot of good movies. **Re-Animator** was the first Stuart Gordon movie that I saw, knowing nothing about it. Do you know where I first saw **Re-Animator**?
SG: No.
JL: On Hollywood Boulevard with some Hammer film or some… not a Hammer film. When did it come out?
SG: '85.
JL: I don't know, it was some British horror picture. It was a British horror picture and **Re-Animator**. Bob Greenberg told me… Do you know Bob? Do you remember him?
SG: Yeah, yeah, yeah, of course [Bob Greenberg was an SFX technician who helped get **Re-Animator** a producer, Brian Yuzna].
JL: I'd been making **Spies Like Us** and I came back and Bob Greenberg was having these barbecues. His card said "Bob Greenberg, special effects and barbecues". He was quite an interesting guy he died very young.
SG: I know, suicide.
JL: I didn't know.

SG: He was an old friend of mine.

JL: I had no idea.

SG: It was Bob that stepped aside and let me direct **Re-Animator**. It was amazing. I mean, I would never do that for anyone. It's incredible. He had this gig to direct this film. Brian Yuzna was going to finance it and the front end was sort of falling apart. They had all the money ready and they had no project and so Bob said, "I've got this friend Stuart Gordon…"

JL: Stuart comes from Chicago, the Organic Theater where people like Bill [William H.] Macy and Joe Mantegna worked.

JR: We recently had a new **Re-Animator** DVD release over here and there's a extra about that…

JL: Good, good. So I went to the movie theatre because Bob Greenberg said you've got to see **Re-Animator**. So I went and I was so delighted with it. I thought it was so funny and I didn't expect it to be quite so smart a movie. Nor quite so outrageous. I wanted my wife Deborah to see it and she said, "You know I don't like that stuff." And I said, "Please see it." When she did she said, "Oh John, this isn't a horror film, it's Dada!" She loved it… Anyways, Stuart who I now know and has acted for me in a film – I quote him all the time. There's a famous Hollywood quote by Sam Goldwyn, I think: "Less is more." He was arguing with William Wyler about something and he said "Less is more." But Stuart says, "Less isn't more! MORE IS MORE!"

SG: I've got a new one. "More is not enough!"

JL: I like the other one better, "More is more." Because I use it all the time.

JR: I'm kicking myself now because I almost brought for you as a gift a copy of a book that I wrote about zombie cinema…

JL: [shouting in mock outrage] Well why didn't you? You prick, I want it!

JR: Well, I didn't think it was appropriate… But now I'm sitting in a room with the man who directed **Re-Animator** and the man who directed **Thriller**…

JL: What's it called?

JR: It's called *Book of the Dead*…

JL: *Book of the Dead*?! I *have* that book. You know what's not in it that really aggravated me? Jack in **American Werewolf**! He's the living dead, he's rotting, but no one ever refers to him as a zombie… It's never brought up. You mentioned **Thriller**… That's a terrific book! It's selling all over the United States. You know, I'd have been much more respectful of you had I known…

JR: It normally works the other way round when people find out I've written about zombies. They're far less respectful…

JL: My son Max who's a very clever writer and he goes to the University of Miami, he wrote **Deer Woman**, this thing that Stuart and I are involved in for the 'Masters

of Horror' series. His now-ex girlfriend was obsessed with zombies. She was this Goth chick. Last summer George Romero asked me to go to this festival he was involved with so that – he said – he'd have someone there he could talk to. So I'm sitting there having dinner with George Romero and I realized who I should call. So I called my son: "Max where's your girl? Put her on the phone." She talks to George Romero and it was like she was talking to the Christ. She was *so* excited to be talking to George Romero. Max was like, "Dad, you have no idea what you've just done!" So I bought her that book and I bought one for me.

SG: Do you know, I read this thing that said more people in America are worried about being attacked by zombies than they are about germ warfare. That's really true.

above: Zombie or ghost? Jack comes back in **An American Werewolf in London**.
opposite: John Belushi on promo material for **National Lampoon's Animal House**.

JL: Yeah, but zombies are real. Germ warfare… Where did you read that? He pulled that out of his ass! Do you know the other thing Stuart did that nobody knows about Stuart? He created **Honey, I Shrunk the Kids**.

SG: I did it with Brian Yuzna who's on his way here now.

JL: Really? I don't think I've ever met Brian Yuzna… Your hair is getting long Stuart. I'm not joking. You have more hair than the last time I saw you. *[SG's head is not what one would call hirsute…]*

SG: Well I've been on the road, I haven't been able to take proper care of it. I've been in Italy for the last week. I was at a film festival, the Joe D'Amato Film Festival.

JL: Another horror film festival?

SG: Yeah in Tuscany. They did a retrospective called 'Gordon mania'. They showed nine of my films.

JL: The only retrospective I ever had besides Torino was in Edinburgh. It was freezing. It was like, "Here would you like some haggis?" You get Tuscany, I get Edinburgh. Anyway, Jamie, ask me something.

JR: Sorry to interrupt.

SG: No, sorry to you.

JL: But you know I'm sorry you didn't bring me your book. I really do have it. There's pictures of your movie in there, Stuart. It's very successful I think.

JR: We didn't think it would successful. I thought there were only a few weird people like me who wanted to know about zombies…

JL: But zombies have become… It's interesting because George Romero is given a lot of credit for this but he copied a movie called **The Last Man on Earth** with Vincent Price. Those were his zombies.

JR: Vampire zombies.

JL: In terms of proletariat just people in suits and ties wearing normal clothes, that kind of blue-collar zombie thing started there. I don't want to take away from **Night of the Living Dead**, that's a great film. The movie that I saw and thought, "What's wrong with everybody?" was **28 Days Later**. I enjoyed it but it got rapturous reviews in the States with people saying it reinvented the horror movie. All I could think was, well, these people haven't seen very many horror films. The whole thing of being fast – I've seen lots of zombie movies where they're fast.

SG: Like **Re-Animator**!

JL: Exactly. **28 Days Later** and the remake of **Dawn of the Dead**, the first ten minutes of both movies are *great*!

SG: I liked **28 Days Later**. I thought it was great.

JL: I liked it for ten minutes.

SG: No, I liked it all the way.

JL: Listen, you know me. I enjoy movies, but I was so taken by the first ten minutes that I was crushed by the rest. Anyway, let's go.

We were talking about **The Blues Brothers**. *Roger Ebert called it the Sherman Tank of musicals…*

Well, Roger Ebert is the Sherman Tank of film critics! **The Blues Brothers** came out of Dan Aykroyd's passion for rhythm and blues and black American music. John Belushi and Danny had performed as Jake and Elwood Blues in Toronto a couple of times. I thought there's a movie in these guys, these low-life recidivist white-trash guys and we could have some really great music in it. We made a deal with Universal before there was an album or anything so there was a development team in place around the time Danny did **1941**.

Then Steve Martin said, "Why don't you guys open for me at the Universal amphitheatre for my stand-up gigs?" So we made a deal with Atlantic Records and we put together the band for the movie: The Blues Brothers Band. That was recorded live at the amphitheatre and that album went triple platinum. *Triple platinum!*

That's how the movie got made so quickly. It was a unique situation. Dan Aykroyd had passion for this music and a desperate desire to focus attention on these artists who weren't working. In '78 the biggest acts were the Bee Gees and ABBA. It was all disco. To this day it's embarrassing because people say, "How did you get

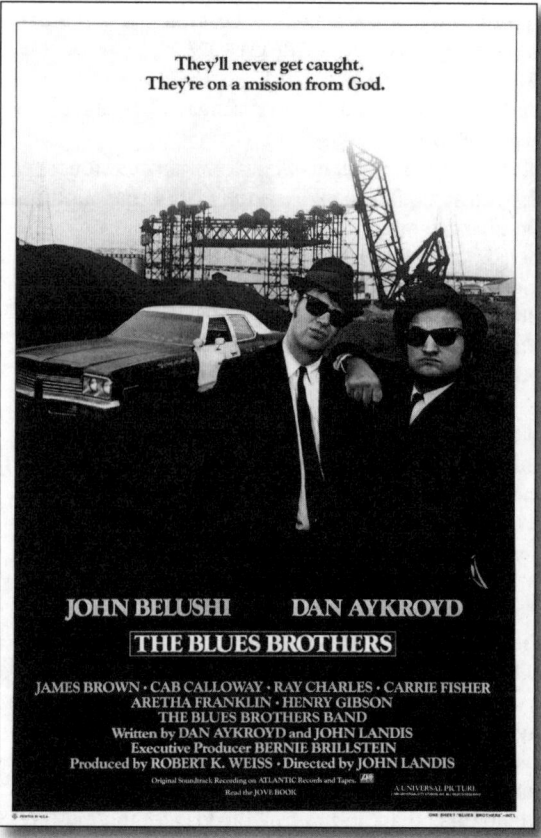

22

Aretha Franklin or James Brown in this movie?" and you don't want to say, "Well they weren't doing anything else, they were thrilled to be in the movie." It's a unique case where John Belushi and Dan Aykroyd exploited their own celebrity to focus attention on other acts.

To give you an idea of how outré this was: when we made it MCA/Universal had the biggest record company around. They refused to take the soundtrack album because they said, "No one's going to buy this." So Atlantic Records, a so-called 'black label', took the movie soundtrack and they wouldn't put John Lee Hooker on there! I had to fight with them and they finally said, "He's too black and he's too old." The picture was a great success and did what it was supposed to do and that's right down to Danny Aykroyd. But the whole mission from God thing was me making fun of Danny. Because he really was on a mission from God.

Then you did a sequel, but by that time you'd lost Belushi. What motivated the return to the Blues Brothers?

Well we wrote a sequel but John's drug use got so bad I said, "John, you clean up or you're gonna die. I'm not going to work with you like this." What happened was he did die and the sequel died with him. More than a decade later Danny started over with these restaurants called House of Blues. He started performing as Elwood and the band got back together. He realized he loved to perform and he said, "We've gotta do a sequel." I was like, "Danny, John's gone…" In any case we made a deal for a sequel with the studio and then the studio's management changed. It's basically New Hollywood, something Stuart will tell you about. It's a very different place to work. All the companies now are bigger than countries. They're teeny subdivisions of huge multinational corporations. NBC Universal is this much [holds up thumb and forefinger] of General Electric. They make atomic submarines, they make light bulbs. They make big business. Warner Bros. is this much of Time Warner. Sony's an electronics company. The bottom line has changed. It's no longer enough for the majors to make a movie and make a profit; they're not in that business. They're about the stock market of the parent company. They will spend $300 million on **Spider-Man 3** because they know that when that movie opens it will knock up Sony stock two or three points, which is a billion dollars. It's a very different business than it was. They're not that interested in giving filmmakers opportunities. They want to make safe things. Look at the quality of the products…

What was my point? Fuck it, I *had* a point. So the new management didn't want to make the movie. So Leslie Belzberg [producer on **Blues Brothers 2000**]

said, "If we give them no reason to shut us down, they can't. Just say yes to everything." Which we did.

The first thing they wanted was a PG rating, which meant we couldn't swear. Taking the profanity away from the Blues Brothers is like cutting their nuts off. There's no nudity, no blood in the first one but it's an R-rated film because they swear, a lot. It's essential to their characters, they're low-life recidivists. The second thing was the character John Goodman played they found unacceptable for various reasons. He was rewritten. Then they said, "You've got to have a child in it because nobody knows who the Blues Brothers are." It was like, "*What?!*" The bottom line is, it was my first really bad experience with a studio. Ultimately, Danny said, "It's not about us, it's not about the movie, it's about putting these people on film. We're documenting them!"

Who was in **The Blues Brothers**? Ray Charles, James Brown, Aretha Franklin, John Lee Hooker, Cab Calloway. Who's in **Blues Brothers 2000**? Well, *everyone else*. Danny's big insistence was that these people are going to die. And bizarrely, since then, Junior Wells has died, Little Walter, Grover Washington Jr. have all died. Billy Preston has died. Ten people in the movie have died. He wasn't wrong! I have very mixed feelings about the finished movie. By the time they'd finished raping the script, John Goodman had no character. He's just standing there. But on the other hand it's got spectacular music in it from Eric Clapton to Bo Diddley and Blues Traveler. The music is great and almost all of it was recorded live, which is amazing.

*OK, so that was the horror of working with a studio. Tell me about your own great horror movie **An American Werewolf in London**. We're here in Piccadilly Circus, which seems kind of appropriate.*

I liked making that movie very much. It was an easy movie to make because I was signing the cheques. It was a picture I'd written in 1969. It's now become a documentary about what Piccadilly Circus used to look like. It was a pleasure. When you've made as many movies as I have you never know which picture people are going to say is your best. In Spain it's **Thriller** or **Three Amigos**. In France it's always **The Blues Brothers** or **Trading Places**. Here it's **American Werewolf**. In Japan it's **Coming to America** and in the US it's **Animal House**.

[At which point the harassed PR finally flips out. We've run over time and I still need to get quotes on a few more movies to make the film-by-film list work… Generously, John agrees to reschedule more time for the next day.]

FROM THE DIRECTOR OF AN AMERICAN WEREWOLF IN LONDON

For generations,
the Mafia preyed
on the innocent.

Tonight, someone's
feasting on them.

INNOCENT BLOOD

A movie that goes straight for the jugular.

WARNER BROS. PRESENTS

A LEE RICH PRODUCTION A LANDIS·BELZBERG FILM "INNOCENT BLOOD" ANNE PARILLAUD
ROBERT LOGGIA ANTHONY LAPAGLIA DON RICKLES MUSIC BY IRA NEWBORN EXECUTIVE PRODUCER JONATHAN SHEINBERG
WRITTEN BY MICHAEL WOLK PRODUCED BY LEE RICH AND LESLIE BELZBERG
DIRECTED BY JOHN LANDIS

R RESTRICTED

So, I told you yesterday I only need quick answers to these questions. It's just a short, list type feature. One of your more underrated movies is **Innocent Blood**. *It's such a great idea to combine wise guys and vampires.*

Originally, I had a screenplay *[by Richard Christian Matheson and Mick Garris]* called **Red Sleep**. It was about Vegas showgirls. The premise was Vegas is a city created and built by vampires. All the entertainers are vampires. It was a way of sustaining themselves without drawing attention because they could have humans run the city during the day doing all the shit jobs and the vampires could feed on the transient population at night. But it was wonderful because what it was really about was show-business. It was a brilliant concept. The King of Vegas in the '50s was Sinatra; in the '70s it was Elvis. Now it's Cirque du Soleil. There were musical numbers in it and it was incredibly gory. Warner Bros. were so freaked out, the blood drained from their faces. They were like, "What the fuck is this?" But they were committed to doing a movie with me. So, they gave me this other script, **Innocent Blood**. I quite liked it. It was an interesting script because it's a mafia movie with vampires. As wacky as **Innocent Blood** was, **Red Sleep** was too wacky for them.

   It is a horror picture but it's really supposed to be funny. It's like Martin Scorsese doing a Hammer Film: **Deadfellas**! Did you notice, the entire cast of **The Sopranos** is in it, fifteen years before **The Sopranos**? I think that Robert Loggia is brilliant in it. He redefines over the top. I love the idea of a Mafioso – a true monster – suddenly being given superpowers. I think he's wonderful when he's figuring out who he is. Don Rickles gives one of my favourite lines in all my movies: "Sal, don't murder a cop on my lawn."

Now you worked with Eddie Murphy a couple of times, when he was up-and-coming and when he was a star. Let me ask you about **Trading Places** *first. He was real young then, wasn't he?*

Trading Places was young Eddie Murphy. He was terrific and talented and sweet and funny. He was on **Saturday Night Live**, so I only had him three days a week. Just like John Belushi on **Animal House**. I had terrible fights with the studio about the cast. It developed for Richard Prior and Gene Wilder. When I met Eddie he was 19, he was very excited and collaborative. I had an interesting time on the picture because I had final cut. When I hired Dan Aykroyd *[the studio]* was very angry. Danny made a picture called **Doctor Detroit** that bombed. So conventional wisdom – which is always wrong – said Aykroyd's no good without Belushi. It's what they said about Dean Martin when he split up with Jerry Lewis.

above: Anne Parillaud plays a vampire that takes on the Mafia in Landis's under-appreciated **Innocent Blood**.

Danny's a wonderful actor. He's nuts, he really is crazy. He's wonderfully warm-hearted and generous. He's a conspiracy theorist nut. He believes in UFOs, ghosts, all that shit. At one time he was studying to be a Jesuit priest. When he was in the Jesuit seminary he was doing burglaries and truck hijackings with this gang. Danny's epiphany would be to commit a crime and arrest himself, that's what one of his girlfriends once said.

Was Eddie Murphy very different to work with on **Beverly Hills Cop III***?*

Eddie and I fell out on **Coming to America**. Years later I got a call for **Beverly Hills Cop III** and I was like, "Sure, but who's playing Eddie Murphy?" I still think it was Eddie's way of apologising. I met Eddie and I said, "If we do this you can't be late, you have to do this *[properly]*". He was absolutely professional but the script was terrible. The original **Beverly Hills Cop** script is not very good but the director Martin Brest made it funny. Literally everything funny in that movie is not in the screenplay… it was all improvised. So I thought I could do that with Eddie. What I learned was Eddie was terribly jealous of Denzel, Sam Jackson, Wesley Snipes. He wanted to be an action star. On the second day of shooting I said, "Why don't we do this?" He said, "John, I really don't think that Axel Foley would do that, that's a wise-ass thing to do." I was like, "Yeah, that's the definition of Axel Folly." He said, "I'm a man now. Not a wise-ass kid, I'm a man." It was clear he wanted to be an action star. In the movie, you actually see Eddie approach jokes and step around them. He basically wanted to be an action star. So it's an odd movie. It's like a comedy cop thriller without the comedy. There's some funny stuff in it but it's a weird movie.

Jamie Russell is a freelance film journalist, author and broadcaster. His work has been widely published in many magazines including *Sight & Sound* and *Total Film*. He is most well-known to horror film fans as the author of the best-selling FAB Press publication *Book of the Dead: The Complete History of Zombie Cinema*.

Sugar and Spice and All Things Nice

Sweet Movie and the Films of Dusan Makavejev

Carl T. Ford

The '60s and '70s counter-culture revolution introduced a number of significant filmmakers to the stage of world cinema. Perhaps the most controversial of these is Yugoslavia's Dusan Makavejev, whose taboo-breaking movies of the '70s, **WR: Mysteries of the Organism** (1971) and **Sweet Movie** (1974) achieved notoriety and faced censorship problems for their unabashed expression of sexual politics and violence. But whilst **WR: Mysteries of the Organism** was highly praised amongst critics and hailed as one of the most subversive masterpieces of the decade for its eroticised politics that propose sex as the ideological imperative for revolution, **Sweet Movie** was reviled by both the press and filmgoers (despite achieving some success in Israel and Italy) and outlawed in several countries (including South Africa, Britain, and Canada). The scandal caused by the film meant that Makavejev would not make another for seven years.

Born in 1932 to Serbian parents in Belgrade, Dusan Makavejev became hooked on cinema after seeing Disney's **Snow White and the Seven Dwarfs** – a film that he felt had been "made for [him], for [his] generation." He studied psychology and began writing film reviews based on film society screenings of British '30s documentaries and classic Russian silent films. In 1953, Makavejev made the first of a series of 16mm films, **The Journey to Old Yugoslavia**, supporting his personal film projects with finance obtained from several documentaries produced for Yugoslav companies. **Spomencima Ne Treba Verovati** (1958) was the first to feature sexually-charged scenes of seduction, and was banned in its home country for five years as a result. His first full length feature, **Man Is Not a Bird** (1966), mixes fiction and documentary footage in a tale that includes all the staples and motifs seen in the director's later work: sex between beautiful women and sleazy men, improvised scenes involving local performers (in this case a hypnotist and a snake charmer), violence, vivid location shooting, and the use of monumental architecture to dwarf and fascinate the characters. **Love Affair, or the Case of the Missing Switchboard Operator** is the tale of the title character's trysts with a sensitive rat catcher that leads to disaster. The film plays with time, juxtaposing scenes of the denouement with the past and inserting revolutionary film clips to illustrate the contrast between communist pomposity and the lives of ordinary people destined for malevolence. His next feature, **Innocence Unprotected** (1968), is a witty re-cutting of scenes from an earlier 1942 movie (of the same name) secretly made, during the Nazi occupation, by an acrobat called Dragoljub Aleksic; it concerns a young girl whose stepmother wants her to marry someone other than her lover, Aleksic. The original was notable for being the first Serbian film with sound but had found itself censored by the Nazis for its whimsical shots of the male body that included lengthy close-ups of Aleksic flexing his muscular form and indulging in egocentric acrobatics.

Makavejev's most accessible film, **WR: Mysteries of the Organism**, takes the writings of sexual psychologist and philosopher Wilhelm Reich (famed for his 'orgone box', which he alleged could be used to cure diseases such as cancer), integrated with footage of Reich and his wife alongside interviews with friends and family, and mixes them up with controversial excerpts from the Soviet-made Stalin feature **Pitsi** (aka **The Vow**, 1946) and Nazi atrocity footage. The result serves as a paean to Reich, a plea for sexual liberation ("Comrade-lovers, for your health's sake, fuck freely!"),

WR: Mysteries of the Organism

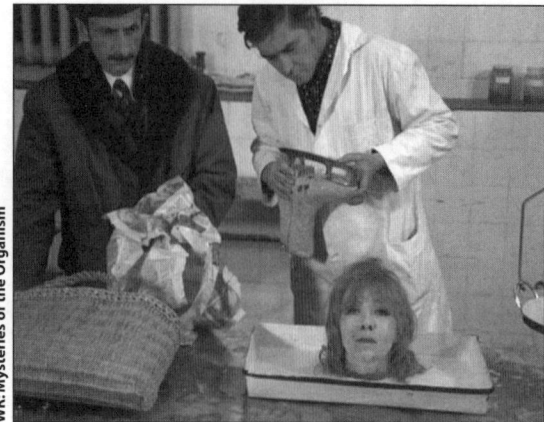

WR: Mysteries of the Organism

It is precisely the inclusion of children in some of **Sweet Movie**'s sexually charged scenes that outraged the authorities in several countries. Filmed in Canada, France and Holland, this bizarre satire on insanity, debauchery, and the 'sweet' joys of the flesh has one intention: to shock. The film features two parallel storylines. One concerns a 1984 Miss World winner and her abduction by a cult of mad hedonists while the other tells of a sailor's death at the hands of a psychotic sexual revolutionary in a bed of sugar…

The film opens to a shot of a peasant woman singing in operatic tones, "On the mountain top I see something black. Is it cow shit or my beloved?" The film cuts to a bizarre Miss World 1984 final sponsored by a chastity belt company, and four contestants find themselves undergoing a virginity test. A female judge, looking like a cross between Barbara Cartland, Mary Whitehouse, and The Bride of Frankenstein, extols the virtues of the chastity belt and its ability to dampen the sexual appetite in women, "If not controlled and kept at bay, wild impulses will turn everyone into beastly animals." Up for grabs is $50,000,000 and marriage to a Texan billionaire.

and an anti-war film. Outrageous visuals include a plaster cast being made from the penis of the editor of American sex magazine *Screw* and a Soviet figure skating champion who beheads his girlfriend with one of his skates following ejaculation. The film ends with its sexy star Milena Dravic announcing to a crowd of assembled Yugoslav workers and peasants, "Fuck merrily and without fear! Even the smallest child will tell you that the sweetest place is between the legs!"

A gynaecologist arrives on a unicycle and proceeds to examine the finalists. Miss Southern Rhodesia starts to get turned on and it soon becomes apparent that she is not a virgin, the bare breasted Miss Congo attempts to seduce the doctor by treating him to a head massage with the aid of her feet, whilst muscular feminist Miss Yugoslavia proceeds to wrestle the judges and beat all the men present to pulp. It is left to the beautiful Miss Canada (Carole Laure) with the "sweetest" vagina to carry off the trophy and marry Mr. Dollars (John Vernon).

The action switches to the second tale. A boat named Survival, bearing the figurehead of Karl Marx, cruises into Amsterdam's harbour crewed by Capt. Anna Planeta (Anna Prucnal) and her singing troupe of revolutionaries. A passing sailor (Pierre Clémenti) spies the boat and is smitten by its sexy captain. He pursues the craft on his bicycle through several canals and is eventually invited aboard.

Back in Canada, Mr. Dollars is preparing to bed his new wife; he meticulously cleans his teeth, washes himself and strips down to his white boxer shorts that bear patterned cherry prints. He strips his wife and washes her with antiseptic, removes his shorts,

reveals a golden penis and urinates over her, giving new rise to the term golden showers. The scene is intercut with stock footage of the Niagara Falls.

We discover that the Dutch sailor hails from the Battleship Potemkin. Captain Planeta tells him, "Those who starve know how to make love." The two then proceed to make love upon the boat's ladder, much to the enjoyment of a cheering crowd on the edges of the canal (most likely, consisting of unsuspecting

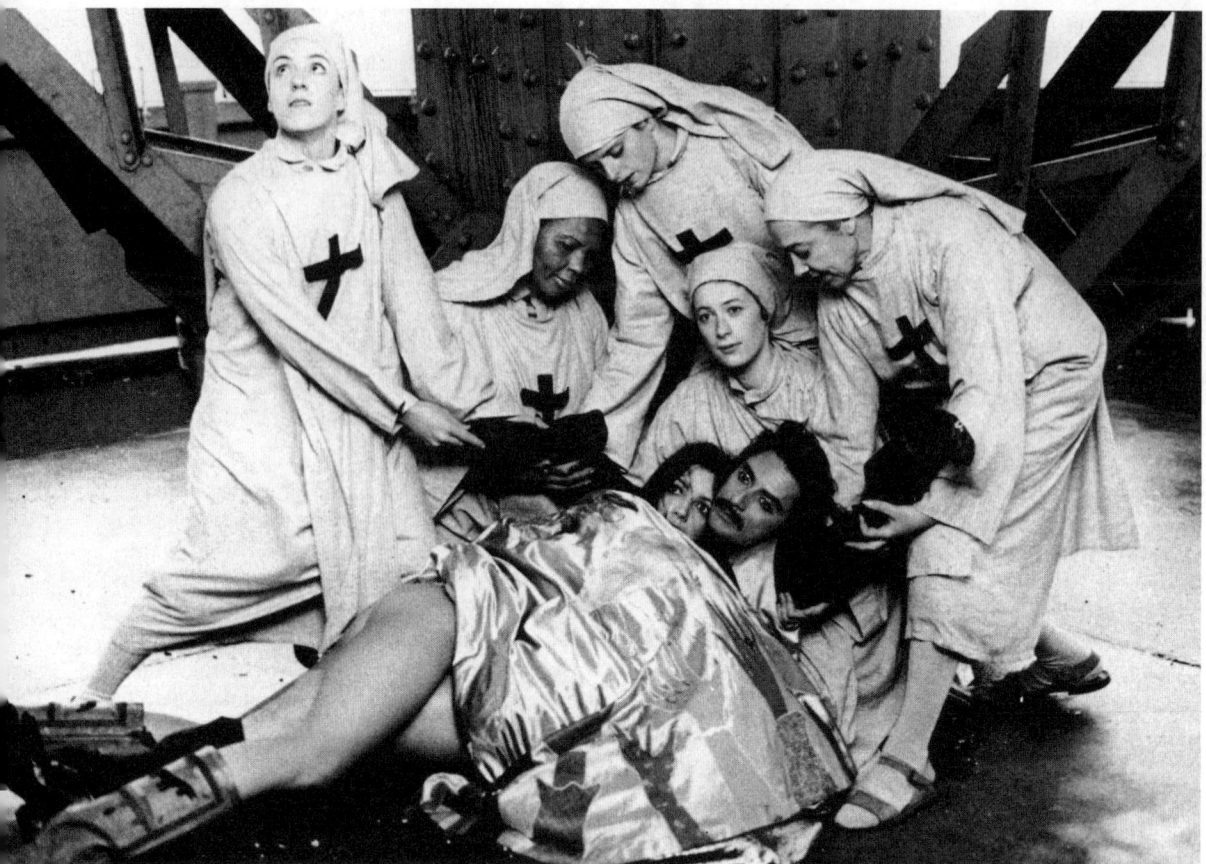

members of the public out in force to witness the filming of Makavejev's hilarious antics).

Poor Miss World is not having things so good. She is thrown into a swimming pool, then dragged out by a muscle man who cages her within a huge plastic milk bottle. She is forced to perform sex acts for him, then packed into a suitcase and sent by plane to Paris.

The revolution is getting into full swing aboard the Survival where the naked sailor is being bathed by several female revolutionaries and informed that the boat is full of corpses. We are then treated to the first of a series of newsreel documentaries spliced into the main action that foreshadow events within the disparate narratives: in the forest of Katyn thousands of corpses – the result of a murderous spree by Nazis – are discovered. This is followed by a brief shot of the Dutch sailor diving into a vat of sugar.

The virginal Miss World escapes from the suitcase and finds herself at the foot of the Eiffel Tower, where a live performance by greasy camp rock star El Macho (Sami Frey) – imagine a nightmarish combination of Demis Roussos, Freddie Mercury, and Renato (of 'Save Your Love' infamy) in a Sombrero – is being filmed. "I'm a wild stallion. Hoofs of gold, flying mane. Looking

for the feast with a thrusting sword", he warbles. The superstar is captivated by Carole Laure's semi-clad charms and ignores an adoring crowd of women that include a group of nuns. It is not long before she is deflowered beneath his black cape. She is obviously a shag to boast about down the local, because an ecstatic looking El Macho passes out on the job. The couple awakes in a chef's kitchen surrounded by camera-clicking nuns, an army of fans, and the entire kitchen staff who witness a doctor announce that the pair have become inseparable as they are suffering from "love cramp"… "It happens to dogs too", he explains. They finally 'come' apart as El Macho entertains all and sundry with another terrible song whilst Miss World cracks eggs on top of her head.

A group of prepubescent boys are enticed onto the boat by Captain Anna with the offer of lollipops. Then they are lured to the hull where thousands of sweets housed in old printer type cases await them. Anna appears in a virgin's bridal gown worn back to front in order to display her breasts, and starts removing her garters, stockings, and gloves and drapes them over the excited kids. The scene ends with the young boys joining her for a round of sweet sex.

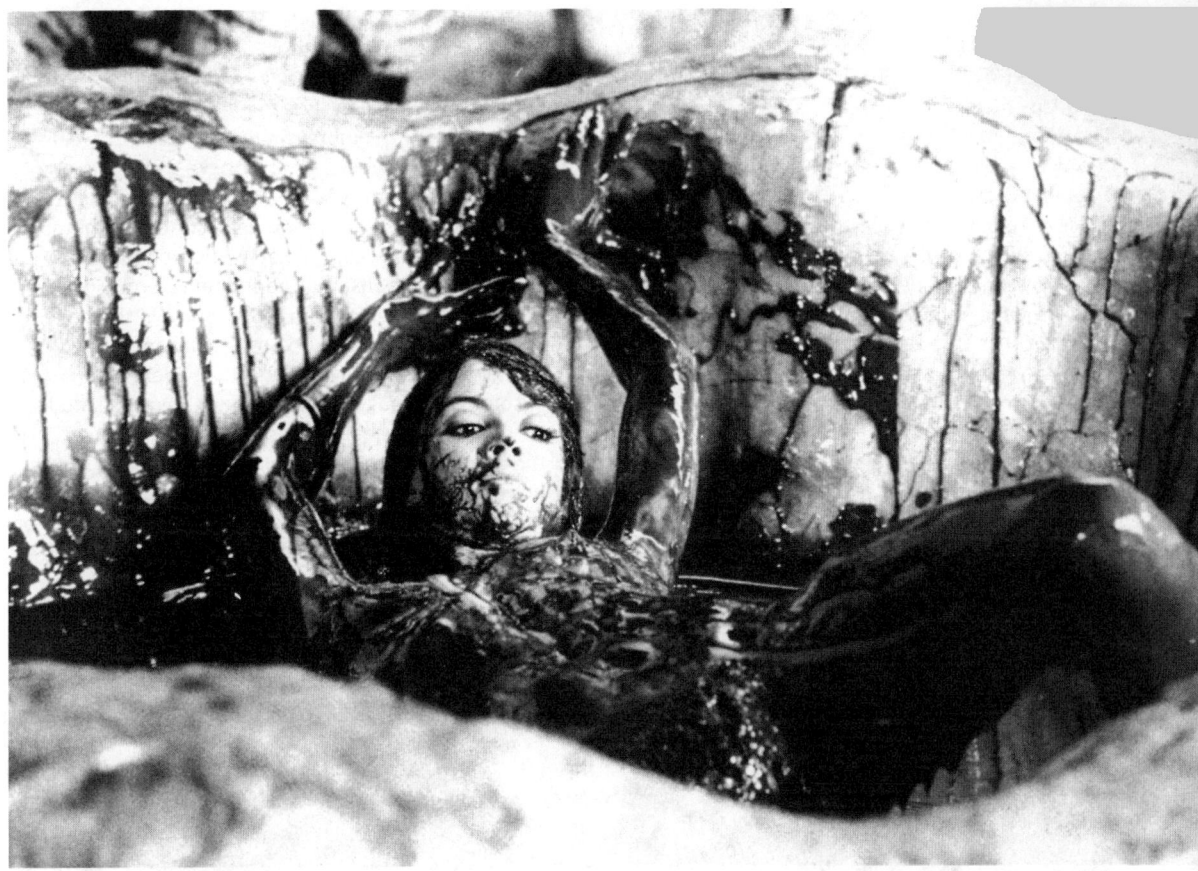

Miss World seems to have lost her mind and is put into the care of the 'Therapie-Komune', an insane sect of sexual deviants who indulge in infantilism. There follows a lengthy food orgy that some viewers may have difficulty watching. The commune members scoff from plates with their hands, spit food, vomit, have sex, and urinate over each other, before participating in a defecation contest with the resultant faeces recycled on food plates. This gross episode is accompanied by further archive footage entitled "Physical Drill for Health's Sake. Hygienic Gymnastics in which a doctor from Berlin massages babies and swings them about by their feet."

The food orgy climaxes with shots of a delirious obese man being pummelled in the stomach. Understandably, he pukes up its contents whilst a topless, shaven haired woman rubs herself up and down his chest. The assembled crowd massage him until he urinates over himself and is then smothered in flour. The scene ends with everyone dancing naked.

Aboard the sugar boat, Anna and the sailor make love in the sugar bed as a white mouse runs over them. They drink coffee and make love once more. Anna viciously bites her lover and he bleeds profusely, but

before he can react, she pulls a knife and disembowels him beneath the sugar. Puddles of blood rise to the surface and he dies. A tracking shot by the side of the boat reveals an angry crowd as the corpses of the sailor and all the young boys are pulled ashore. The Dutch police arrive and arrest the screaming captain and her female crew. We witness another group of young children assemble on a bridge to survey the scene.

The film closes with a sequence in which a naked Miss World bathes in a vat of chocolate until she drowns. We cut to war footage of the Nazis examining the decomposed corpses of their victims, interspersed with shots of the Dutch children in body bags lying on the bank. They slowly rise from their sugar coated death sheets and gaze at the camera.

A surreal combination of the darkest elements of early David Lynch, Pasolini, and Pythonesque visuals, **Sweet Movie** has to rate as one of the most original and disturbing movies of the '70s. Despite the fact that there is no story as such, and little characterisation, the film lingers in the mind long afterwards. It is stylishly directed and the scenes are highly fetishised. The striptease performed by Anna Prucnal, when she goes into Hansel and Gretel mode, is particularly erotic.

The film is all the more thought-provoking when one realises that this scene ought to be shocking. Fascinating visuals abound, the Survival bearing the head of Karl Marx sailing through the canals is a marvellous image, and equally absorbing is the scene in which Carole Laure covers herself with chocolate.

Roger Ebert of the *Chicago Sun-Times* believes "the movie defies criticism while it seems to demand it". The fact that **Sweet Movie** lingers in the mind is not purely down to its outrageous visuals: the film is quite a roller coaster when it comes to engaging the emotions, too. As Makavajev has stated, "**Sweet Movie** will not be afraid of looking like a dream and will permit many oddities. It hopes to fling you from horror into joy, and then again, quite unexpectedly, to jerk tears out of you." As well as probing the idea that madness is often the key to survival in a loveless world inhabited by greed and war, the film investigates the paradoxical way in which 'sweetness' interacts in our daily lives: the seductiveness of sugar and candy, the allure of sex and fetishism, how its delights can lead to addiction, and the manipulation of/by sweetness that can result in tragedy and corruption.

Makavejev, therefore, must have been delighted that the movie stirred up such controversy. It has been alleged that the star, Carole Laure, stormed off the set, an act that led to the Canadian authorities banning the movie. In Amsterdam, the owner whose houseboat was used as the Survival instigated a lawsuit against the director when he learned of the film's planned finale. When the judge announced a ruling was due in eight days' time the plaintiff realised that Makavejev would, by then, have shot the scene and fled the country. So he boarded the ship with a group of friends in order to take control of things himself. Makavejev immediately ordered his camera crew to film the ensuing chaos, that resembled an anarchic final reel from an Errol Flynn swashbuckler. Yet my favourite tale concerns the Italian dubbed version of **Sweet Movie** (over which Pier Paolo Pasolini presided). A few years ago the popular Italian current affairs weekly *Espresso* magazine learned of the film's controversial history and decided to put the question of whether the film constituted art or exploitation to its readership. An amazing 600,000 copies of the film on videotape were shrink-wrapped with the magazine and sent out to its readers. There it is, this outrageous movie, so rarely seen in the UK, probably shelved next to a copy of a Fabio fitness video in any number of Italian charity shops.

Carl T. Ford edited the cutting-edge exploitation cinema magazine *Unrated*.

above: Maverick director Dusan Makavejev at work, making the original controversial 'Serbian Film', **Sweet Movie**.

Psychos versus schoolgirls: Alan Birkinshaw's **Killer's Moon** disregards all notion of political correctness, becoming an exploitation cinema classic in the process.

The Killing Moon

An Interview with Alan Birkinshaw

Xavier Mendik

The Horror Show event (organised by Harvey Fenton of FAB Press in association with Norman J. Warren) took place at Riverside Studios in London during June 2001, to mark the publication of the book *Ten Years of Terror: British Horror Films of the 1970s*. One of the guests present was the cult British director Alan Birkinshaw, who introduced a rare cinema screening of his 1978 exploitation classic **Killer's Moon**. The film explores the disruption of a rural community and its inhabitants following the escape of four crazed mental patients who are undergoing 'radical' forms of therapy as a way of dealing with their inner rage. Directed by their psychiatrist to use their dreams as a forum to vent their most sexually aggressive urges, the four patients rape, mutilate and torture the locals (and their pets), believing their own actions to be part of a crazed dream scene.

In true exploitation fashion, the focus for the inmates' mayhem takes place in a deserted hotel where a group of teenage schoolgirls have taken refuge for the night. This plot device allows the film to wander an uncomfortably thin line between archaic St. Trinians style antics and more contemporary forms of softcore titillation that were popular in Britain at that time. Birkinshaw was himself no stranger to these milder forms of 'English' eroticism, having previously directed **Confessions of a Sex Maniac** (1974), a breast and buttock laden farce about an architect attempting to model his designs on the female bosom. However, in **Killer's Moon**, the combination of blood, breasts and British seaside humour makes for uncomfortable viewing, a factor confirmed by the film's graphic on-screen violence and acts of implied animal cruelty.

Birkinshaw later directed another minor cult hit with the jungle adventure film **Invaders of the Lost Gold** (1981). Here, B-movie regulars such as Stuart Whitman, Harold 'Odd Job' Sakata and British 'bad boy' character actor Edmund Purdom (literally) rubbed shoulders with grindhouse regulars such as Laura 'Black Emanuelle' Gemser, while searching for hidden World War II treasure in the Philippines.

In this exclusive interview by Xavier Mendik, Birkinshaw discusses sex, suffering and the reasons why the bottom fell out of British exploitation cinema at the end of the seventies.

Xavier Mendik: Today's event is a celebration of 1970s British horror and exploitation cinema. What are your memories of working in this era?

Alan Birkinshaw: Well, it was all good fun. I think that these days, too many people take themselves too seriously, which we didn't back then. I know that there is a lot of money involved in making a film, but people should remember that we are all here today and gone tomorrow.

Some of the themes of 1970s British horror: urban alienation, harsh and inflexible state institutions and repressive family structures imply that they should be taken seriously. Would you not agree?

I don't really know. You never quite know how these things are going to turn out and quite often it's a surprise when they turn out brilliantly and then people start looking for wider themes or social issues in them which perhaps were not intentional, but may be present anyway. Obviously you went out to make the very best film that you could; most of them didn't work and occasionally one of them did, but most of these films were made for fun. We came up with an idea and wrote a script, some people liked it and put some money in, I put some of my own money into these projects and off we went.

*We tend to associate you with British horror cinema, but your first film was a sex comedy entitled **Confessions of a Sex Maniac**.*

We did that purely because I had a friend who was prepared to put some money into various film projects. We had no idea what kind of film to do, so we thought we would test the market by doing an exploitation picture. If it worked, then we would come up with a bigger budget and a different type of film so that we could start to work up towards the films we really wanted to make.

The film seems to have had a curious production history; some reports even suggested that it was mistaken for a hardcore porn movie?

I think the French distributor who brought the rights for the film cut in a sequence that he had shot himself, which was far more explicit than the original cut I had prepared. Someone I know was in France and they saw the film advertised, popped into the cinema to see it and was quite bemused by what they saw in it! However that wasn't anything that I shot, and that wasn't even the intention of the film.

The most obvious difference between hardcore and the British sex comedy is that the former celebrates the excesses of male potency while the latter just pokes fun at phallic 'failure'. Would you agree?

(*Laughs*) Yes, and that comic failure was exactly how Britain was during the seventies! You could have sex, but you couldn't have 'serious' sex. So what you had to do was dress it up, and the best way of doing that was by playing it for laughs. So you would have these scenes of naked girls running in and out of a room, so those who wanted to see naked flesh could see, but it was dressed up in a kind of comic farce, so that you could get it past the censor.

*Yes, but the theme of lacklustre male leads seems also central to **Killer's Moon**, which was screened at the festival today. The hero's opening line is to comment on his own flagging libido to his girlfriend.*

Yes, this was because that particular line was written by a female. I should tell you that my sister is Fay Weldon and she wrote some lines of dialogue for the film.

*The 1970s saw the decline of Hammer horror and a very different kind of British horror movie took its place. Would you classify **Killer's Moon** as part of that new trend in British horror?*

Well, we certainly tried to make a contemporary horror picture and it nearly came off! I wouldn't claim that it was the greatest film in the world, but there were some quite good things in it. There were things in that film that did work, while others clearly didn't. If I was going to do that movie again I would do it entirely differently.

The film's scenes of animal cruelty offended many people, particularly the implication that one of the maniacs has chopped a dog's leg off.

Well of course this did not really happen, I would never allow it to happen, as I love animals. In fact we owe a great deal to the dog as he managed to get us a great distribution deal! The dog had quite a history, having been given a 'doggy VC' for his courage. Apparently, he used to be a pub dog whose owner was being held up and the animal's leg was wounded when it went to protect his master. We needed a dog with a leg missing for the film and initially I intended to use the dog I had at home. So I tried tying this dog's leg to make it look as though it was missing a limb, but it couldn't run and kept on falling over! So then I had the bright idea of getting this three-legged dog instead. Anyway, when it came to publicising the film's release, we knew that the press would love a good 'animal story'. So we had a photo-call at Peppermint Park, which was a fashionable cocktail bar in London. At 10:30 in the morning, the press turned up and we had arranged the dog sitting in the bar with a cocktail drinking straw in its mouth surrounded by all the girls from the film. So the photographers took all these fabulous photographs and the story appeared in *The Times*, *The Telegraph* and all the other newspapers. At the time we were playing in just a couple of the cinemas in the ABC circuit, but following the publicity, the exhibitors gave us a full release. So we did quite well out of the dog!

top right: Alan Birkinshaw at work on the **Killer's Moon** campsite murder scene.
opposite: No anmals were harmed during the making of this film...

*Although clearly made on a very tight budget, **Killer's Moon** does contain a number of stylistic flourishes, such as unconventional point of view shots.*

Yes, well I stated off my career as a television cameraman, and I recognise that in any film the use of camerawork is of the utmost importance. The cameraman for **Killer's Moon** was one of the best cameramen around at the time but he had a slight drInk problem! This was a real shame because he had worked on some really big film projects and also had been taken off other big film projects because of his drinking habits. I met him by accident and liked working with him a lot.

*Beyond the film's visual 'look', the soundtrack to **Killer's Moon** also had an experimental feel. How did that evolve?*

The bloody chaos of **Killer's Moon** was orchestrated by Alan Birkinshaw, who can be seen swinging an axe in the production still shown on this page (*bottom left*).

I do think the music for the film is very interesting, though once again we did not have the budget to create a totally effective soundtrack. As a result, there are points in the film where the music is not quite right. At certain points some of the music seems terribly old fashioned. I looked at the film the other night, after not having seen it for more than ten years. What struck me was that some of it was incredibly creaky, but other sections of it are quite fun and unusual.

The film did tend to bracket your work very much within the more disreputable end of horror cinema. How comfortable did you feel about this?

Why I made a horror film was that it seemed to be the next step to making the sort of films that I would rather have made, which were thrillers. If I had a cinema hero, it was Roman Polanski and at the time I guess that's the direction I would have liked to have gone in. Hindsight tells me that if that was the sort of film I wanted to make, then that's what I should have been making first. Instead I went down this rather circuitous route.

*Moving away from **Killer's Moon**, you are also remembered in cult circles for your jungle action adventure film **Invaders of the Lost Gold**. What are your memories of this film?*

It was a real experience! I was writing that every night before we were shooting it the next day. The script that we had originally was so appalling that we couldn't shoot it! So every night I was re-writing the movie and would have to present the actors with a new script the next morning, and retrospect tells me that this is not the best way to make movies.

The film featured American actor Stuart Whitman, who was in many exploitation movies during the seventies.

Stuart Whitman, I thought, was a brilliant actor. I really enjoyed working with him. We had the opportunity to make this film and there we were in the jungles of the Philippines, shooting in the same locations that **Apocalypse Now** had left a year earlier, with quite a few of the people who had been in that film.

*Did the film's location make **Invaders** a difficult shoot?*

Most definitely so. Every single thing that could conspire to go wrong during filming did. Every single day we couldn't film, sometimes for up to eight hours at a time for the most extraordinary reasons. The dialogue was so bad it had to be constantly re-written, which lead to rows with the actors and some of the local actors we had to use were terrible. There were a couple of people that were so bad that I had to remove them only to find that this caused political problems in the area, so then I had to give them different roles! After all that, we ran out of money at the end of the shoot and I took over the UK rights in order to salvage the picture. However, in the end it only got a very limited release.

Beyond your use of Stuart Whitman, the film employed the talents of character actor Edmund Purdom, who often appeared as a British bad guy. What was he like to work with?

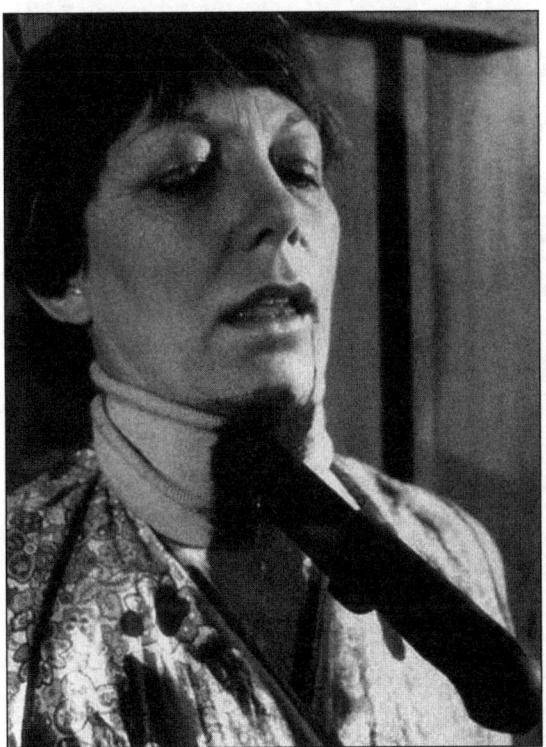

He was a really lovely guy. You have to remember that Edmund Purdom was a big name leading actor at one time. When he was in **The Egyptian**, it was one of the biggest films of all time. The problem with Edmund was that he was a bit eccentric and also he was a bit of a sex maniac! He got hounded out of Hollywood for seducing a studio head's wife or daughter, so he disappeared to Rome where he lived for over thirty years. Because he went on to work extensively in the Italian film industry and also in another language, there was never anyone to really guide him with these roles. As a result, all his performances appear to be a little over the top.

*Just to close, the FAB Press book **Ten Years of Terror** ends with a discussion of the slow death of the British horror film over the course of the eighties and nineties. Why do you think this form of genre cinema declined after its seventies heyday?*

The bottom did drop out of the horror film market. Partly this was because it became so difficult to get money to make films; there were all sorts of strange people coming in with the authority to say "yes or no" to the funding of projects. Around 80% of films made in England at the time didn't even get shown in this country, and those that did were pretty dismal anyway. There are some filmmakers who are clearly gifted, the first film that they make turns out to be wonderful and they are off and running. For the rest of us lesser mortals it's just hard graft!

This interview originally appeared in the online journal Kamera.
Xavier Mendik is the Director of the Cult Film Archive at Brunel University.

Un film de
Carlo Infarcelli
EASTMANCOLOR
NORMA PRESENTA
Super
Decameron 3
Erótico
DADO CROSTAROSA · ORCHIDEA DE SANTIS
GABRIELLA GIORGELLI · MALISA LONGO · ELENA PARKER

Boccaccio's Bastards

The Decameron from Pop to Porn

Kier-La Janisse

Of all the imitators of Boccaccio (1313–1375), perhaps the most perplexing are the film directors who created the 1970s genre of Italian sex comedies known as the 'Decamerotics'. Styled after Boccaccio's masterwork, these films summed up the ideological catastrophe that had befallen Italian cinema in the years leading up to the death of Pier Paolo Pasolini in 1975; they were cheap, commercial, shallow, and yet they made a mark on the history of eurotrash that still resonates today.

The catalogue of cinematic Decamerotica is in excess of 50 titles (many more if you count those based on *One Thousand and One Nights* or tales of ancient Rome, as some scholars do). Most of these movies were made in the few short years from 1971–1975. The production of the Decamerotics began officially in 1971 with Gianfranco De Bosio's **La betìa ovvero in amore per ogni gau denza ci vuole sofferenza** (aka **In Love, Every Pleasure Has Its Pain**) – which had actually been made prior to Pasolini's **The Decameron** but suffered distribution issues that left it unreleased for some time – and closed their doors in 1976 following the release of late descendants like Romano Gastaldi's **Fra' Tazio di Velletri** (1973) and Lucio Dandolo's **Quant'è bella la Bernarda, tutta nera, tutta calda** (1975). And as popular as they were in Italy, these films were even more so in export territories like France and Spain.

The definition of Decamerotica in its strictest sense requires that it is a medieval sex comedy based on stories from Boccaccio's *Decameron*. But in reality the term was applied to any vulgar costume comedy regardless of whether or not it was based directly on Boccaccio's text, set in the Middle Ages or the Renaissance, or episodic in structure. Still, the majority of the Decamerotics descend – if only nominally – from novels of the 15th Century, inside the temporal spectrum between the beginning and the end of the Renaissance, and staging tales more or less structured around love, jealousy and hypocrisy, and which generally sought to castigate vice and exalt virtue (especially that of an erotic nature). Aside from Boccaccio, other writers whose texts were popularly plundered for Decamerotic substance were Geoffrey Chaucer (1343–1400), Ruzante (Angelo Beolco , 1502–1542), Pietro Aretino (1492–1556) and Cardinal Bibbiena (1470–1520).

There are several reasons behind the proliferation of Decamerotica in 1970s Italy, one of which was the spillover of the sexual revolution into mainstream cinema. Although strictly Catholic, Italy nevertheless was one of the first countries to mass-produce erotic films, and the 1960s were full of them; sex films were commonplace in Italy by the end of the 1960s, but while extremely lucrative, they would not enjoy the mainstream acceptance that this type of film went on to enjoy a decade later. Italy was host to a plethora of cinematic imports that, while predominantly softcore, stimulated the imaginations of those who would provide the new wave of Italian exploitation filmmaking in the 1970s. As Italian film production was at its lowest ebb at this time due to the emigration of many Italian directors and producers, it is not surprising that cheap sex-comedies became the order of the day. But why the Decamerotics in particular? Was it because Pasolini had furnished an adaptation of Boccaccio's masterwork as the first installment of his 'Trilogy of Life' in 1971? Luchino Visconti, Federico Fellini, Vittorio De Sica and Mario Monicelli may have planted the idea in the minds of those directors whose efforts would later be scoffed at as "nibbling at the erotic crumbs which fell from the lavish banquet tables of Pasolini" (Manlio Gomarasca, *Nocturno* 10), with their participation in **Boccaccio '70**, a composite film that nevertheless has no direct connection to the seminal Boccaccian text. Despite its title, it was made in 1962, nearly an entire decade before the Decamerotics took over, but it's worthy of note because it shows the undeniable influence of *The Decameron* on popular culture. The Mario Monicelli story is missing from many prints of the film, which is unfortunate since he was the only one of the quartet to continue with period comedies (**L'armata Brancaleone** (aka **For Love and Gold**, 1966); **Brancaleone alle Crociate** (aka **Brancaleone at the Crusades**, 1970)), providing a necessary link between **Boccaccio '70** and the Decamerotics that proliferated a decade later.

The Italians were also under a lot of pressure to equal competitive American output, and the American director Sam Phillips had produced a cheap *Decameron*-inspired sex film in 1970 – a year before Pasolini's more reverential contribution to the newly-emerging

Boccaccio '70 was actually made in 1962, almost a decade before the first of the true 'Decamerotics', but it's noteworthy for demonstrating the influence of *The Decameron* on popular Italian culture.

subgenre – called **Love Boccaccio Style**, which starred infamous porn star John Holmes. Whether or not Phillips's film was a direct influence on the Italian sexploitation directors can only be speculated upon. But the hallmark of Italian cinema had always been its direct relationship to real life, and the Decamerotics were no exception. For the real impetus behind the 'Decamerotic' explosion one must look at the bigger picture – namely, the similarities between 1970s Italy and that decade's medieval counterpart in which Boccaccio's *Decameron* had its genesis.

The Decameron was written in the years immediately following the Black Plague in Florence in 1348. Boccaccio scholar Thomas Bergin maintains that Boccaccio's intent was primarily a diversional one; neither to "inspire nor to instruct" (not all scholars will agree, especially linguists who admire Boccaccio's obvious familiarity with various forms of literature, both courtly and otherwise, including the fabliaux and macaronic poetry), and points out that of the 100 tales contained therein, 67% have some sort of sexual conquest as their narrative focus. This would make *The Decameron* a fruitful source for 1970s exploitation filmmakers who were more than familiar with the text from high school, where it undoubtedly functioned as a form of softcore entertainment for their pubescent

masturbatory fantasies. But by this time, *The Decameron* had been recognized as a masterwork of literature, and reading it was compulsory in an academic setting; it was only in the 19th Century that the book received the scholarly reappraisal that forever placed it in the academic curriculum. "It was widely read before it was deemed worthy of criticism or even mention," says Bergin, "and criticized long before it was truly appreciated." Critics and scholars of Boccaccio's own time either ignored *The Decameron* or thought it vulgar and reprehensible, and it was only partially validated after the vernacular was deemed acceptable for serious literature with the humanism characteristic of the Renaissance. *The Decameron* was even included on a list of prohibited books officiated by the Council of Trent in 1560. Nevertheless, the book remained popular, and spawned several imitations, including Franco Sacchetti's *Trecento novelle* (1399) and, of course, Chaucer's own homage to Boccaccio, *The Canterbury Tales*.

The Italian political and economic arena has always been less than consistent, and this must be considered when looking at the cultural context for both the text of *The Decameron* and the 1970s Decamerotica. 14th Century Italy was characterized by mercantile expansion, and by the accumulating wealth of the newly emerging urban bourgeoisie. These new-money merchants may not have had the traditional land-wealth that brought them the class of nobility, but they were nevertheless an integral part of Italian society at the time, as they were the prime example of a newly developing social mobility that had been previously unheard of. Where the text found its audience was in the newly emerging merchant class, whose customs and way of life figure largely in *The Decameron*.

The Decameron was extremely popular among the middle and upper-middle classes (such as the Bardi, Buondelmonti, Acciaiuoli and Cavalcanti families, for example), and of all the copies of *The Decameron* circulating at that time, two thirds of them belonged to these families, and many would be copied by hand so as to increase circulation even further, as well as being disseminated orally. Boccaccio was the first to recognize the historical importance of the merchant class, witnessing their vitality first-hand, as his family had long been bailiffs for the powerful Bardi family. He imparts to these merchants the same literary dignity that the medieval tradition gave to nobility. But while these companies are a constant in Boccaccio's text, they are not always portrayed in a positive light; Boccaccio also calls attention to their limits, that the 'ragion di mercatura' demanded that they be inhumane and petty when circumstance called for it. While their activity created an economic stimulus for certain cities on the whole – such as Boccaccio's Florence – this only managed to cement the gap between rich and poor, and to make the poor less noticeable, even though there were almost 20,000 paupers in Florence alone.

For any kind of centralized government, such as the Holy Roman Empire, Italy was a force to be reckoned with; it was impossible to control, and this was only enhanced further by the move of the Papacy to Avignon. The Guelphs (pro-papal) and Ghibellines (pro-imperial) had reduced most of central Italy to anarchy, and the part of Italy known as the Papal States was subject to vicious feuds between local families, so then-Pope Clement V (1305-1314) chose to move the papacy to Avignon to be away from the factional strife prevalent in and around Rome. This move may have guaranteed more personal security for the Avignon Popes, but did little for their esteem in the eyes of their Italian subjects. The only consistent thing about Italy's political situation was its inconsistency: constant factional strife, civil wars instigated by feudal barons, and later uprisings of the populo minuto (lower economic classes) made any kind of central government weak, if it existed at all. In Florence, political power was especially unstable, with favour shifting from one party to the next almost overnight.

Business in the 1340s was in a slump, which was especially hard-hitting given the successful commercial activity of the decade before. The Hundred Years' War had disrupted trade with Northern Europe, and the violence between Guelphs and Ghibellines had escalated (even though there were not actually that many Ghibellines in the Florence of the 1340s), which further disrupted trade and diplomatic dealings. To complicate matters further, the populo minuto became a concern in the 14th Century as well, and towns where industry thrived were always hotbeds of class struggle characterized by worker unrest that would reach a zenith in the famous Ciompi uprising of 1378. But while the Guelphs and Ghibellines (who were almost exclusively from old, noble families) were busy feuding with each other, this only worked to create more social mobility for those not of noble birth, which Boccaccio seized upon for his characterization in *The Decameron*. "Writers such as Boccaccio played a vital role for Florence in suggesting how new forms of moral excellence might be exemplified by characters of humble or intermediate social status", says Thomas Bergin. Moreover, in detailing how a group of young Florentine men and women could go unchaperoned to the country – which would be considered quite unacceptable at the time – Boccaccio "shows how the communal, self-governing instincts of Florentine polity are kept alive through a period of social collapse, [which] makes a significant and timely contribution to this civic ideology."

The Italian political and economic situation in the period directly leading up the Decamerotic wave was no less chaotic. To properly examine a cinematic trend in Italy during the 1970s, one must necessarily regard its cultural context as more far reaching than the mere few years that the Decamerotics reigned supreme. Apart from the neorealist movement of the immediate postwar period, the 1960s had been Italy's richest period of cinematic output; it was the time of Fellini, Antonioni, and Pasolini – and it was Pasolini himself, Italy's national poet, who would be instrumental in creating the Decamerotic wave. But integral to this tsunami of cinematic talent was an underlying criticism that would escape few areas of Italian output. A short-lived economic boom in the early 1960s gave rise to a massive increase in film production, both for the domestic and international markets; chances were being taken, and new voices were being heard. Competitive pricing in Italy led to collaborations with American companies, which soon ranked Italy second in the rostrum of cinematic superpowers.

This consumer-driven atmosphere was soon interrupted by another generation of angry voices, young filmmakers whose utopian ideals challenged "not only the power of money, not only capitalism, but also the bureaucracy, the hierarchy, the division of labour, the atomization, and the mechanization of city life." (Edgar Morin). In March of 1962, Amintore Fanfani formed Italy's first centre-left government, consisting of the Christian Democrats (DC), the Social Democrats (PSDI) and the Republicans (PRI). Although the Socialists (PSI) were still not included in the governmental coalition, the time was becoming ripe to do so; a coalition with the Socialists would break down the latter's ties with the Communist Party, which would only strengthen the power of the Christian Democrats

above: **Brancaleone alle Crociate** (aka **Brancaleone at the Crusades**, 1970), is a notable link between **Boccaccio '70** and the Decamerotics.

and help centralize a very unstable government. The Christian Democrats had the support of most of the industrial sector – most notably that of Fiat, Pirelli and Olivetti – in their decision to eventually include the PSI in government, for two reasons: "The advent of central government planning seemed more likely to enhance than to impede the growth sectors of the economy, and the presence of the Socialists in government would, they hoped, help to diminish the growing tension in the Northern factories." (Paul Ginsborg) In December of 1963, under the leadership of Aldo Moro, the plan was implemented and a new coalition was formed that included the Socialist Party for the first time since the war.

The new coalition and its reform programme – which purportedly included tackling the issues of poverty in the South and the backwardness of much Italian agriculture – was not as unanimously supported as the Government had hoped. Many former members of the PSI withdrew their support, believing that the Socialists had 'sold out' in allying with the Christian Democrats. Between 1962 and 1968 the centre-left governments had failed to materialize their promises, and to respond to the multiple needs of a rapidly changing Italy, resulting in large scale workers' strikes and a student protest movement that outlasted any of those elsewhere in Europe.

One of the reforms put into place by the new coalition was the introduction in 1962 of compulsory secondary schooling. Because of this, the number of enrolled students going on to University had more than doubled by 1968, but the facilities did not exist to accommodate this mass expansion. There were not enough textbooks, classrooms, nor enough competent teachers. Apart from these obvious material reasons for student upset, many students were disillusioned by the values that accompanied the 'economic miracle' of the late '50s/early '60s. They turned to the revival of Marxist thinking that was taking hold of Italy at the time, as well as traditional Catholic beliefs which, although not entirely in agreement ideologically, "provided part of an ideological background in which the values of solidarity, collective action, and the fight against social injustice were counterposed to the individualism and consumerism of 'neo-capitalism'." (Paul Ginsborg) Congruent to the student protests in France, Germany, Japan, Mexico, and America, Italy's disaffected youth took to the streets in 1968.

Pasolini's attitude toward the student revolts was divided. Although ideologically in agreement with many of the same principles, he believed that the students were behaving like spoiled brats, upholding an attitude of moral superiority; he believed that the students, for the most part, were merely caught up in

the excitement of the protest, but that they were all from well-off families and really had little empathy for the underprivileged. "You have the spoiled faces of your fathers", he remarked in his 1968 poem *Il PCI ai giovani*, "I sympathized with the policemen! Because policemen are sons of the poor." He thus saw the 1968 protest movement as a mock-civil war by which "the students placed their bourgeois world into crisis in order to reify it." But soon, the protesters' monitory outcry against consumer excess saw its fruition in reality: Italy's 'economic miracle' soon metamorphosed into an economic crisis as the decade drew to a close.

A worldwide recession in the early 1970s had profound effects on the Italian situation: Italy was host to substantial workers' strikes and inflation, and the overpopulation in the cities due to emigration from the countryside, and from the South to the North, made for increased social and political tension as well as – according to Pasolini biographer Naomi Greene – "hastening the destruction of regional customs and dialects, of age-old patterns and beliefs." Most of Italy's talent pool – the directors and producers who made Cinecittà the 'Hollywood on the Tiber' that it was – were leaving to work in America and other countries abroad. Splinter left-wing terrorist groups, angered at the moral laxity of Italian society – and the inability of the Communist party to properly address it – advocated the use of violence in protecting the people from the corrupting force of capitalism. The 'sexy seventies' ushered in a new era of fierce anticlericalism as well, but there was little the Vatican could do about it in practical terms, and it had to sit by as the precursory anticlericalism of *The Decameron* was immortalized on celluloid. By the mid 70s, the legalization of divorce and abortion were under way; but rather than feel a sense of victory in this new 'tolerance', Pasolini instead saw it as a grand humiliation, as an attempt to hegemonize all that was polemic in order to subdue it:

> "Everything has been overturned now... the progressive struggle for the democratization of expression has been rendered obsolete by the decision of the powers that be to allow vast (and equally false) tolerance... the 'reality' of innocent bodies has been violated, manipulated, and tampered with by the power of consumerism."

Pasolini's lighthearted **The Decameron** (1971), the first volume of his 'Trilogy of Life', was a surprising turn after the pessimistic **Medea** that preceded it by two years, but in keeping with his own assertion that he was "a force of the past", he turned again to an ancient text for inspiration, in this case "to celebrate the base

instincts of a not yet corrupted humanity: the first of which is sex." But the book's necessary context – the plague – is decidedly absent from Pasolini's somewhat obscured window into the middle ages.

In the place of Boccaccio's framing story, Pasolini has inserted one based on *Decameron* 6:5, in which he is a disciple of Giotto (in Boccaccio's text, the character is Giotto himself) who posits himself among poor monks as he creates his masterpiece. And yet this removal of a representation of the Black Death in favour of a framing story more flattering to his image is ironically counteractive to his assumed 'ideology'; Boccaccio exalts those not of noble birth because they have an inner nobility that does not require a pedigree, and demonstrates this by showing how they uphold their values even in a time of pestilence, when the world they know is rapidly disintegrating. As such, perhaps it would have been in Pasolini's interest to leave Boccaccio's framing story intact. However, Pasolini's decision to cast himself as a disciple of Giotto is not a superficial detail, but one that betrays Pasolini's persistent interest in the populo minuto. Accompanied by his lawyer Forese da Rabatta (played by an actor who would later appear in **The Ribald Decameron**), who is described in Boccaccio's text as "being deformed and dwarf-like in appearance" but "a jurist of such great distinction that many scholars regarded him as a walking encyclopedia of law", both men arrive at the monastery in such a humble state of atire that they could easily invite criticism that they were not who they claim to be. This is Pasolini's characteristic self-affiliation with the lower classes. It was the reality of the populo that the work of Giotto reflected. "The populo", writes Lauro Martines, "by its sustained attacks on authority, altered the political and social organization of the old urban space and changed the disposition and the thrust of values. This in turn, had a pervasive effect on imaginative literature, political thought and historical writing… the art of Giotto and his followers would have been impossible without the psychological stamp of the populo." Medieval Art Historian Margaret Miles points out that "Giotto enjoyed tremendous success as a revolutionary painter, whose paintings discarded the stiff, authoritative figures dominating medieval art at the time in favour of humanized and humble figures." It is also important to note that Giotto was known for the low positioning of Jesus's loincloth in his crucifixion paintings, which coincides well with the repeated crotch-shots evident in Pasolini's film.

Also unique to Pasolini's **The Decameron** is the special emphasis placed on the city of Naples. While the corresponding tales in the original text *do* take place in Naples, Pasolini seems to have deliberately

this page: The drama and spectacle of Pasolini's seminal 1971 film **The Decameron**.

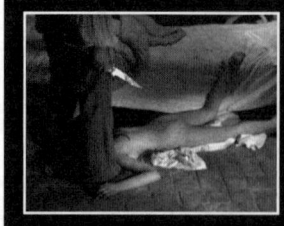

above: Nudity and violence abound in Sergio Citti's outrageous and politically scathing epic **Storie scellerate** (aka **Bawdy Tales**, 1973).

chosen Neapolitan stories (such as *Decameron* 2:5, 1:1, and 7:2, as well as Pasolini's added framing story) because it was his hometown, and due to the city's mixed reputation for both popular resistance and underworld violence. **The Four Days of Naples** (aka **Le quattro giornate di Napoli**, 1962), co-written by Pasquale Festa Campanile, who would go on to direct two proto-Decamerotics) depicts Neapolitans as heroes through its portrayal of the WWII-era Neapolitan rebellion against invading Germans, while films like Umberto Lenzi's **Violent Naples** (aka **Napoli violenta**, 1976) and Lucio Fulci's **Contraband** (aka **Luca il contrabbandiere**, 1980) would later immortalize Naples as a city owned by protection rackets and policed by unorthodox cops whose protocol was entirely their own. Nevertheless, in Pasolini's fourth tale (*Decameron* 1:1), the unrepentant criminal Ciapelletto (Franco Citti of Pasolini's **Accattone** and **Edipo Re**) sings, "Naples! My beloved Naples! Those who lose you love you…" It was also in Naples that Boccaccio met the painter Giotto, whose personality Pasolini appropriates for his role in **The Decameron**.

Pasolini contributed to another Decamerotic, Sergio Citti's **Storie scellerate** (aka **Bawdy Tales**, 1973), which starred Pasolini regulars Franco Citti and Ninetto Davoli and featured a script co-written by Pasolini. **Bawdy Tales** stands apart as one of the more politically scathing (largely clerical) commentaries of the bunch, as well as having production values that put the others (including Pasolini's, ironically enough) to shame. The film also manages to capture the spirit of Boccaccio's original text far more aptly than many of the Decamerotics, despite the decision to move the narrative from a medieval context to the 18th Century. The storytellers in this instance, Citti and Davoli, demoralize Catholicism and brag about their various attacks on the church while taking a crap beside each other. "Sometimes it's rough, sometimes it's smooth", says a third man who joins them in their faecal endeavor, "just like life." They take turns telling stories that involve an M.G. Lewis-type priest who beds a parishioner's young wife, a married woman

who indiscriminately frolics with all the young men in the town whilst her older husband is asleep, a shepherd who tricks another into having sex with a sheep, a poor couple who take on a ménage-à-trois with a lusty and wealthy geriatric, and a young man who dupes an unchaste priest in order to partake of the Church's bountiful foodstuffs. While the stories are not adapted from actual tales from Boccaccio's *Decameron*, they carry a degree of Boccaccian wit not seen in many of the other Decamerotics, which are merely content to exploit the sexual content of the original. **Bawdy Tales** also happens to be the most overtly violent example of the genre, with several graphic castrations, decapitations, hangings, whippings, multiple stabbings, and one man is even hung upside down from a tree, his abdomen split open, while his murderers partake of his flesh for dinner! All in all, Citti's film is a lush and colorful example of the genre, and is successful in its vindication of the hypocrisy of the clergy, as well as trivializing spiritual matters in favour of more human interests. What also binds Citti's film to Boccaccio's text is that the narrators have an escapist purpose to their storytelling; just as Boccaccio's narrators weave their tales to escape from the devastation of the Black Death, Citti's tell their stories to escape their miserable, poverty-stricken existence and, subsequently, their pending execution. Even on the scaffold, awaiting their sentence, they stand laughing blindly at their own scatalogical stories.

But in the end, Pasolini knew his attempts at escapism had been futile, and that "the anarchic power of sex had been domesticated as soon as it was transformed into a consumer good like so many others." In June of 1975 he wrote the *Retraction of the Trilogy of Life* (published posthumously), that renounced the series for this very reason.

Although Pasolini's 'Trilogy of Life' is credited as the major driving factor in the proliferation of the Decamerotic genre, among the prototypes for the Decamerotics – through their unconventional use of language and hilarious situations – are

L'armata Brancaleone

Mario Monicelli's **L'armata Brancaleone** (1966) and **Brancaleone alle Crociate** (1970), which proved the commercial viability of the epochal costume phenomenon. Gianfranco De Bosio's proto-Decamerotic comedy **La betìa ovvero in amore per ogni gaudenza ci vuole sofferenza** (eventually released *after* Pasolini's film, in 1971) helped to popularize the costume sex-comedy in a 1970s context, but in the spirit of some more obscure '60s predecessors like **A Virgin for the Prince** (Pasquale Festa Campanile, 1965, aka **Una vergine per il principe**), **The Devil in Love** (Ettore Scola, 1966, aka **L'arcidiavolo**), **The Chastity Belt** (Pasquale Festa Campanile, 1967, aka **La cintura di castità**), and

Zenabel (Ruggero Deodato, 1969). All of these films deal with pseudo-historical plots, and parade their scantily-clad women through farcical tales of wit and cuckoldry. De Bosio's film was not based on *The Decameron*, but on Ruzante's *Comedy Without a Title*, a text that, like *The Decameron*, lent itself easily to the exploitation film genre. A year later, the imitations started rolling in.

1972 was the biggest year in terms of Decamerotic output; of the fifty or so films that fall under the heading of 'Decamerotic', thirty of them were made in 1972. It is clear that these directors found inspiration in the 'Trilogy of Life', but they abandoned Pasolini's complex discourse on sexual liberation in favour of exploiting the commercial aspects of sexual exhibitionism accompanied by a comical touch at once arousing and also a little uncouth. One of the first was Franco Rossetti's **Una cavalla tutta nuda** starring genre It-girl Barbara Bouchet and Aldo Caponi (who can also be seen in Mario Bava's **Rabid Dogs**). Mino Guerrini's subsequent contribution was called **Decameron No. 2 – Le altre novelle di Boccaccio** (although the film's on-screen credits list it merely as '**Decameron**'), presumably intended as a nominal continuation from Pasolini's film of the previous year. The film's tone is moderately respectful: the titles take place over a collage of medieval woodcuts (at least they are supposed to be medieval, but more than likely date from the 16th Century), and although the framing story is not elaborated upon (a group of more than seven men and women sitting around a fire take turns telling stories – there are 6 tales in all – but why they are there, or their reasons for storytelling are not disclosed), the tales are almost verbatim from Boccaccio's text. Unfortunately, this makes the film rather redundant for anyone who has read the original text, its appeal lying only in the B-grade star power Guerrini managed to muster up in the form of Camille Keaton and Mariangela Giordano.

The roles given to both Keaton and Giordano (the latter of whom would later appear in Paolo Bianchini's **Decameron No. 4 – Le belle novelle di Boccaccio** (1972) and Lucio Dandolo's **The Lusty Wives of Canterbury** (1973)) in Guerrini's film reflect the complex sexual politics of the time; both *The Decameron* and the Decamerotics came at a time of sexual revolution, a time when women's roles were undergoing a significant change. The thread connecting all these comedies was the women. The male protagonists' sole purpose was the conquest of these beautiful women, and their licentious intentions sometimes brought rewards, other times punishment. Although subject to criticism from feminists who denounced the exploitative nature of the Decamerotics, the women who starred frequently in these films were revered in a way previously unimaginable for actresses who so shamelessly 'revealed themselves' before the camera. Regulars included Femi Benussi, Malisa Longo, Margaret Rose Keil, Gabriella Giorgelli, Krista Nell[1], and Orchidea De Santis, the latter of whom appeared in so many Decamerotics (often alongside regular co-star Dado Crostarosa[2]) that the *Continental Film Review* labeled her, "that princess of the Boccaccian genre". "It was like working an assembly line", recalled De Santis in the book *99 Women*, "you finish one, next you start another… Decamerotics were our 'daily bread' in those days… the first time I undressed before the camera I certainly was [embarrassed]. But the sex scenes were so farcical that all you were required to do was a sort of grotesque ballet on a haycock, on a bed and so on."

In medieval thought, women had always been equated with the archetype of Eve, with the corruption and downfall of man. But by the 12th and 13th Centuries, woman had been changed into a 'lady'; the cult of Eve gave way to the cult of the Virgin Mary, and according to historian Reay Tannahill courtly love became "the great theme of late medieval literature and the great theme, too, of upper class life." The transformation of woman from corruptor to holy vessel and inspiration was partly due to increased contact with the Arab world via the Crusades and, later, by mercantile expansion. As Tannahill explains:

"Arab women were strictly segregated, Western women scarcely at all. The idea of ennobling love had, in fact, been built on the foundation of the harem's walls, so that the true personality of the beloved woman scarcely impinged on the poet's image of her – and this placed the European male at a serious disadvantage. The unconsecrated spirituality of ennobling love which seems genuinely to have caught his imagination, was far from easy to achieve when its object was not only visible and audible, but as far as it is possible to judge, willing and accessible as well."

Thus the idea of the ennobling, inaccessible woman had its genesis in Southern France, and its troubadours and poets (and their imitators) would spread the new laws of love across Europe. This was a game happily played by the upper classes, and especially enjoyed by women who were married, as it was commonly acknowledged that most married women had lovers (or in the case of courtly love, 'inaccessible lovers') since real love was seen as "a gift freely given", thus excluding it from marriage, which was more or less a business contract. Nevertheless, marriage plays an important role in *The Decameron*, one which Boccaccio uses to examine gender roles in and out of marital partnerships, and to explore the organic nature of human values.

The notion of the 'inaccessible woman' attributed to courtly love would become a popular theme in 'common' medieval literature as well as scholarly or courtly literature – although a moral breakdown in the former was used as a means of comic relief. The fabliaux, or bawdy poems modeled after courtly love poems but lacking all the moral virtue, became one of the most significant literary influences on Boccaccio's *Decameron*, and their resonance would still be felt in the Decamerotic films that came centuries later. The spirit of the French fabliaux is equated with the emergence of a new middle class, as is *The Decameron*, but unlike courtly literature, they are more concerned with individuals beating the system. These poems were part and parcel with the 'commercial revolution' of the 13th and 14th Centuries, periods of unprecedented social mobility. They sought to break the fetters of the impractical idealism upheld by the laws of courtly love, and instead sung the praises of deception and practical wisdom. This celebration of cunning behaviour, coupled with the notion of the 'inaccessible woman' espoused by courtly love, made for many amusing situations in Boccaccio's text, but also provided the reader with a more rounded view of the world by juxtaposing them with the tome's more serious credos.

One of the most popular stories in *The Decameron*, and which features in Pasolini's film of the same name, is the story of Masetto and the nuns (Decameron 3:1)[3]. The conniving Masetto pretends to be dumb, and gains the position of gardener at a local nunnery so that he can bed all the young nuns. "There are a great many men and women who are so dense as to be firmly convinced that when a girl takes the white veil and dons the black cowl, she ceases to be a woman or to experience feminine longings", explains Filostrato in his narration to the story, "…and if they should happen to hear of anything to suggest that their conviction is ill-founded, they become quite distressed, as though some enormous and diabolical evil had been perpetrated against Nature." Nuns were (and are) the epitome of the inaccessible woman – but although many of these women saw chastity as autonomy and willingly chose to be wives of God rather than wives of men, others were young women who had disgraced their family or who were 'locked up' to protect their innocence. It is these latter women who formed the foundation of the erotic fascination with nuns that still has a strong appeal in popular culture today. These women were inaccessible only in appearance, and rumours of their waywardness pervaded contemporary gossip as well as literature.

Another of *The Decameron*'s most popular wayward women is Alibech (Decameron 3:10), a young pagan woman from Tunisia who, when inquiring about how Christians best serve their god, is advised that "the ones who serve God best were those who put the greatest distance between themselves and earthly goods, as happened in the case of the people who had gone to live in the remoter parts of the Sahara." Being a very naive fourteen-year-old, Alibech sets out the next morning by herself toward the desert where, after nearly starving to death, she finally happens upon a reclusive monk named Rustico, who takes her in. Unable to control himself, Rustico convinces Alibech to help him "put the Devil (his penis) back into Hell (her vagina)" in order to please God, and she obliges only too happily. Her newfound Christian fervour soon becomes too much even for Rustico, and he is relieved when she is sought out by a rich young man named Neerbal for the purpose of marriage. "And so young ladies", says the tale's narrator Dioneo (who holds the honour of being the most frequently perditious of the storytellers), "if you stand in need of God's grace, see that you learn to put the Devil back into Hell, for it is greatly to His liking and pleasurable to the parties concerned, and a great deal of good can arise and flow in the process." Mino Guerrini takes a few liberties in his adaptation of the Alibech story for **Decameron No. 2**, which sees Alibech remain in the Sahara to 'serve God' with all the other hermits scattered throughout the desert. And Camille Keaton, who plays Alibech, would go on to 'put the devil back into hell' in numerous other films.

Not surprisingly, the Masetto and Alibech stories were considered the most blasphemous in *The Decameron*, a notion gleefully seized upon by Mariano Laurenti for his film **La bella Antonia, prima Monica e poi dimonia** (aka **Naughty Nun**, 1972), a vehicle for Italian starlet Edwige Fenech (who also starred in Laurenti's **Quel gran pezzo della Ubalda tutta nuda e tutta calda** (aka **Ubalda, All Naked and Warm**), made the same year). Based on Pietro Aretino's[4] *Ragionamenti* (aka *Ragionamenti Capricciosi*, which

above: Edwige Fenech, customarily naked, this time in **La bella Antonia, prima Monica e poi dimonia** (aka **Naughty Nun**, 1972).
opposite: Promotional glamour shots from **Una cavalla tutta nuda** (*top*) and **Decameron No. 2 – Le altre novelle di Boccaccio** (*below*).

above: Malisa Longo bares all in **La bella Antonia, prima Monica e poi dimonia** (aka **Naughty Nun**,1972).
below: Edwige Fenech was an icon of the Euro-exploitation movie scene; here her likeness is used to promote Mariano Laurenti's **Ubalda, All Naked and Warm** (also 1972).

translates as 'Capricious Reasons'), rather than *The Decameron* proper, Laurenti recognized the obvious appeal of wayward nuns as proven by the commercial success of both Pasolini's **The Decameron** and Guerrini's **Decameron No. 2**. But while Laurenti's films have been lauded by Italian film writer Riccardo Esposito as the first "true decamerotic comedies", they are not necessarily the best components of the series. **Ubalda...** for example, is little more than a sex comedy for idiots, with ridiculous costumes (through which Fenech's panties are in plain view), flat lighting, mickey-mouse music courtesy of composer Bruno Nicolai, and none of the wit evident in the original text. And **La bella Antonia...**, commonly considered to be one of the best examples of the genre, found a detractor in the *Monthly Film Bulletin* of July 1973: "the

Edwige Fenech
Pippo Franco

Quel gran pezzo della Ubalda
tutta nuda e tutta calda
un film di Mariano Laurenti

cast struggle feebly to invigorate their parts, the more private of which are mercifully concealed during the hero's countless copulations."

However romantic, the notion of courtly love was not necessarily representative of reality. The moral laxity of the game players led the notorious, misogynist jongleur Marcabru[5] to up the odds by insisting on chastity as a prerequisite for any woman being placed on the pedestal that courtly love awarded her. While the troubadours disseminated songs ostending Marcabru's firm moral standpoint, the game-playing became more and more complex and quick-witted, and probably resulted in more fierce extracurricular lovemaking than anything Marcabru had originally railed against. The Church became concerned over the amount of women's confessions of 'lascivious thoughts', or complaining of having been visited by incubi in the night – demons who would invade their beds and sometimes even impregnate them. But Marcabru's message had taken hold on some levels, and it had sorry consequences for women whose husbands locked up their money and saw no reason why they should not do the same with their wives. Italo Alfaro's adaptation of *Decameron* 7:5 in his film **Il Decameron No. 3 – Le più belle donne del Boccaccio** (aka **The Last Decameron: Adultery in 7 Easy Lessons**, 1972)[6], wherein a jealous husband who keeps his wife under lock and key pretends to be a priest in order to hear his wife's confession, has two objective onlookers providing the commentary (sometimes with musical accompaniment) normally attributed to Boccaccio's narrators:

> Onlooker #1: "He locks his door the way a crusader would secure a chastity belt!"
> Onlooker #2: "He's very jealous, my dear. And the lady he has locked in there leads a life that's dry and bitter. The stupid thing is, she's honest and true as the day is long!"

The seventh day of *The Decameron* deals almost exclusively with domestic space and the issue of control over it. "The state is made up of households", said Aristotle, and thus the conflicts on the seventh

above: Typically bawdy Decamerotic scenes from **Quel gran pezzo della Ubalda tutta nuda e tutta calda** (aka **Ubalda, All Naked and Warm**).
below: A theatrical 'fotobusta' for Italo Alfaro's **Il Decameron No. 3 – Le più belle donne del Boccaccio** (aka **The Last Decameron: Adultery in 7 Easy Lessons**, 1972).

day are microcosmic political ones, especially as marriage was most often arranged with economic considerations, rather than romantic ones, in mind. Furthermore, extramarital adventures in *The Decameron* are often due to a discrepancy in age or social status, and Boccaccio generally elicits sympathy for the unfaithful wife, who is acting out against her husband's inappropriate oppressiveness – especially considering that a sexual relationship was not even always expected between a husband and wife in medieval practice. Boccaccio retaliates against the jealous husband with special vigour in *Decameron* 7:8, wherein Arriguccio, a merchant, marries the much younger Sismonda, who is of the noble class, in order to rise in social status further than his merchant-mobility allows. She takes a lover her own age, who alerts her

at night by tugging on a string she has tied to her toe. Arriguccio catches on, and ties a string to his own toe in order to catch the adulterer red-handed. Meanwhile, as Arriguccio is out chasing her lover, Sismonda orders a servant girl to get into her bed and pose as her, so that when the husband returns to thrash his unfaithful wife, she will not be on the receiving end of his blows. Arriguccio does as Sismonda predicts, beating the young servant girl in the belief that it is his wife, then cuts her hair off and takes it to Sismonda's brothers, stating that, "they were to come and fetch her and deal with her according to the dictates of their family honour, as he had no intention of permitting her to darken his doorstep again." When Sismonda's mother and brothers follow Arriguccio to their marital bed, they find Sismonda without a black and blue mark on her, and a full head of hair, stating that Arriguccio's usual night-time debaucheries probably caused him to have an elaborate hallucination. The family immediately sides with Sismonda, much to the chagrin of her cuckolded husband, and Sismonda's mother rails against "the pretensions of the nouveaux-riches" before kicking Arriguccio out on his merchant-class arse.

Aristide Massaccesi (aka Joe D'Amato, as well as nearly 40 other pseudonyms) amassed almost 200 directorial credits, three of which were Decamerotics directly inspired by the success of Pasolini's 'Trilogy of Life'. The second of these, **Le mille e una notte di Boccaccio** (1972), ran into trouble with the Italian censors due the explicit nature of some of its sex scenes, and after being rejected twice, Massaccesi (credited in the film as Michael Wotruba) was forced to change the title to **Novelle licenziose di vergini vogliose** (which translates roughly as **Licentious Novellas of Lustful Virgins**) before the censors would even look at it again. It was finally released in 1973 under this title, but by that time the Decamerotic wave was already fading. Massaccesi's other Decamerotic (made and released in 1972, and which would itself go on to be plagiarized by Luca Damiano in 1994) had an even longer title: **Sollazzevoli storie di mogli gaudenti e mariti penitenti – Decameron nº 69** (though it went on to be rather more pragmatically called **More Sexy Canterbury Tales** in the UK). "No literary ancestry lies behind the story", says Davide Pulici, "the authors had read Boccaccio back in high school and had the good sense to leave him on the shelf and not try to cloak the profane of the Decamerotic material with the veil of the sacred." While Boccaccio's adulteresses were responding to the abusive or neglectful behaviour of their husbands, Massaccesi's do not necessarily suffer the same fate, nor do they especially dislike their husbands – they merely hunger for other lovers, preferably stupid ones that are easily expendable. Massaccesi's conniving women thrive on the control that Boccaccio grants them on *The Decameron*'s 7th day – the household is their territory, and within that realm, their needs will not be denied. In the first segment of **More Sexy Canterbury Tales**, Maria Piera Regoli stars as Antona, a young woman with a frequently absent husband who takes up with a stuttering sculptor who makes her husband seem fascinating by comparison. Antona is not sex-starved, although her lover might be led to believe that was the case, considering her animalistic sex-play that contrasts sharply with his whiny effeminacy. The lover eventually gets jumped by both Antona and her sister-in-law, who quickly tire him out – at which point they kick him out of the house calling him a "prude", and turn to each other for intimacy. Other tales include similarly giddy male characters, some of whom we only

see in drag (including a young Luca Damiano, who would go on to make red-light Decamerotics of his own over 20 years later), a childish man who is abnormally attached to his mother, and a lustful priest who is forced to castrate himself to escape from a chest in which his lover's husband has trapped him. As such, the film is oddly feminist in nature; while it is the women whose bodies are clearly on parade, their quick-wittedness is on show as well, and they leave their male counterparts in the dust. Allied with Diego Spataro and Massimo Bernardi's Elektra film production company, Massaccesi managed to create some of the genre's most vital and daring efforts, with a parodic edge – a parody of a parody, in fact – as Elektra had previously done to the Spaghetti Western genre with **Scansati... a Trinità arriva Eldorado** (aka **Stay Away from Trinity... When He Comes to Eldorado**, 1972). *Nocturno* magazine writer Davide Pulici maintains that **Licentious Novellas of Lustful Virgins** even went so far as to have "the feel of 'off' theatre, or… cabaret".

Piero Vivarelli's **The Black Decameron** (aka **Il Decamerone nero**, 1972) has little to do directly with Boccaccio's text, save for its similarity in structure and the odd borrowed plot device (although Vivarelli tries to 'catholicize' the Africans by having one of their priests threaten to excommunicate someone). **The Black Decameron** betrays the obsession with African culture (one that has its counterpart in the Arab world of Boccaccio's time) that had permeated the Italian film industry since the release of Gualtiero Jacopetti and Franco Prosperi's **Mondo cane** (1962) and the duo's brutal but far less successful **Africa addio** (1966 – re-released under the title **Africa Blood and Guts** in 1970 to a much more responsive audience), as well as other mondo films such as Guido Guerrasio's **Secret Africa** (1969) and **Africa ama** (1971). But as David Kerekes and David Slater have pointed out in their now-seminal tome *Killing for Culture*, the Italian filmmakers oversaw their subject from a position of supposed racial superiority, as did the audiences who flocked to these films throughout the '60s and '70s. Even Pasolini, a filmmaker removed in the popular imagination from the "low-brow" world of Jacopetti and his colleagues, admitted his deep fascination with the African continent, filming there several times himself. Nor was this fascination an attitude unique to 1970s Italy, having a medieval precedent that is visible in the art of Boccaccio's own time.

As can be seen from much medieval cartography, it was believed that at the edges of the known world (i.e. often defined as what we now know as Africa) existed marvellous races of people that practised bizarre customs and were even more extraordinary in appearance. The Sciopods with their one gigantic foot that shielded them from the sun, and the Blemmyae, headless men with faces on their chests, were familiar figures in medieval art and literature. But they were always on the other side of some implicit or explicit boundary that prevented them from commingling with their European counterparts, lest the latter be 'infected' by the savages. At the center of the medieval world map lay the Holy city of Jerusalem, from which – as implied by the codification existent in such maps – the monstrous races (as they were called) were excluded. Not only did they exist at the edges of the physical world, but "at the edges of God's creation" too; they were so far removed from the center of things as to be practically removed from His sight. The tenuous grasp on what lay outside Europe and the Holy Land provoked polarized reactions from those medieval men and women who heard about the monstrous races. Initially, the sheer distance separating the Europeans from such creatures allowed a benign curiosity. The monstrous races served to make Europeans more comfortable with themselves, and indirectly reinforced social norms. Later, when political and commercial contact with distant lands increased, the monstrous races were pushed out into the 'New World', taking on the form of Indians or wild men. But Africa had never ceased to hold a certain magical charm for the Europeans, specifically the more adventurous ones who sought to immerse themselves in the continent's diverse and disparate cultures – and if the 20th Century cinematic tributes to Africa prove anything, it's that many of Africa's 'admirers' were of Italian origin. The world of the marvellous (i.e. the monstrous races) functioned as an inverted mirror-image of the real world – a reflection that was safe so long as the boundary implied by the mirror was kept in place. In the 20th Century, this boundary was provided by Jacopetti and Prosperi's camera lens, and in the case of **The Black Decameron**, by that of Piero Vivarelli.

With the proliferation these genre movies, loyalty to the source material was becoming less and less important, and any costume sex-comedy or bawdy anthology piece could be categorized under the heading of 'Decamerotica'. One such example is Giuseppe Vari's aptly-titled **The Ribald Decameron** (aka **Beffe, licenze et amori del Decamerone segreto** or **Love, Passion and Pleasure**, 1973) – wherein the poet Cecco Angiulieri philanders his way through the hearts and pockets of medieval Italy, his erotic intentions finally falling on the unwitting Mother Superior of a nearby nunnery. While there are several subplots in **The Ribald Decameron**, they all have Cecco as their guiding force, and his efforts bring the characters together in a cleverly devised montage by the film's close. As such, it can hardly be called an anthology, its only similarity to *The Decameron* being its medieval setting – which, like most Decamerotica, is superficial and inaccurate –

and the fact that Cecco's namesake does appear in *Decameron* 9:4, although his story is unique to this film. The flashy credit sequence and contemporary theme music to **The Ribald Decameron** already indicates a departure from established form, one that Laurenti's earlier **Ubalda…** similarly employed, and whose example would be followed by many of its successors.

One of the few Decamerotics to include a reference to the Plague is Mario Sequi's **Fratello homo sorella bona – nel Boccaccio superproibito** (aka **Roman Scandals '73**, and in some places, humourously, as **Decamoronic**, 1972), which is also unique in its reference to homosexuality in the title, even if the film does not follow through on this promise[7]. The film is set during the "Great Plague of 1330" – which is only one of many historical inconsistencies – but that the Plague figures at all is cause for commendation, since almost every other Decamerotic skips it altogether. The same can be said of Sam Phillips's aforementioned American predecessor to the Italian decamerotic wave, **Love Boccaccio Style**. And yet the Black Death that ruthlessly wiped out 75% of Boccaccio's fellow Florentine population can be considered the single most important factor concerning the existence of *The Decameron*. However, it is rarely addressed in the Decamerotics for the same reason Boccaccio's characters railed against the 'depressing' stories king-for-a-day Filostrato has them tell on *The Decameron*'s fourth day, and one recalls Thomas Bergin's assertion that Boccaccio's text is primarily "diversional" in nature. While perhaps not subject to a deadly pestilence, 1970s Italy had problems of its own, that were the result of radical changes in economy, politics, societal values and expectations that mirrored those surrounding the Plague years of the 14th Century. The Decamerotics were a generation's means of survival, both economically and existentially.

Aristide Massaccesi must be acknowledged as a guiding force behind the exploitation explosion of the 1970s that almost single-handedly kept Italian cinema afloat. He was an experienced and respected cinematographer, considered one of the best in Italy even by the likes of Fellini and Visconti, but he was also a capitalist who knew how to make successful and cheap pictures that would employ those in the industry whose careers had been put on hold by the recession. "They had to be good to make a film in two or three weeks", remarked actress Malisa Longo of the '70s exploitation directors, who, like Massaccesi, looked at their product primarily as a commercial venture, "…those Decamerotics had so much dialogue,

above: **Canterbury proibito** (1972) was made by Italo Alfaro, who also directed **The Last Decameron: Adultery in 7 Easy Lessons** the same year.

action, camera movements and so on, and it took skill and great technical knowledge to shoot them." Technical skill is something Massaccesi was no stranger to, despite his lack of ideological integrity. "He is truly an amazing cameraman," said fellow Italian director Alberto De Martino in an interview with Peter Blumenstock and Christian Kessler in *European Trash Cinema*. "It is sad he went into a very strange direction as a filmmaker because he is so talented and could do so much more… Aristide is no longer interested in any ideals, he is just serving the market." Massaccesi was one of the foremost voices in the Decamerotic genre, and his influence could still be felt in the early 1990s when Luca Damiano approached him to collaborate on another string of Decamerotics – this time of a more hardcore persuasion. Of the four 'Decameron X' titles that resulted from this collaboration, Damiano's **Witty Stories of Whoring Wives and Cuckolded Husbands** was the first to be released on home video. "As much as the limited dimension of hardcore ends up making any product ugly," writes Manlio Gomarasca in *Nocturno* 8, "and despite the way the predominance of sex scenes and the poverty of ideas and situations end up suffocating and overwhelming the stories, which are already risky, the Decamerotic genre lived (in a way) its last season thanks to this handful of 'red-light' films, which flashed like a meteor through the washed-out hardcore market in which everything is used up and disappears in the space of a few months in the dusty rooms of the 'sexy shops'. Who would have said that starting from Pasolini we would have ended up on the sabre-like member of Christoph Clark? Life is strange."

The influence that Boccaccio's text has had on contemporary literature and film cannot be underestimated. As a seminal tome of an often maligned and misunderstood era, *The Decameron* held a magnifying glass up to the value systems inherent in a complex society, providing humour, enjoyment, and a speculation on contemporary morals that sees the common man win out in the end. While often

referred to as a text "lacking morals", *The Decameron*'s tales show a pattern leading from vice to virtue: but its virtue is not that of a dusty nobility; it is that of the active citizen who, with good intent and sharp wits, can overcome even a catastrophe as dehumanizing as the Black Death. It is easily fathomable how a text as celebratory of human survival instincts would be so adored by a public wallowing in the overwhelming chaos of its recent history. *The Decameron* still gets internationally adapted for the page and screen, and in Italy the Decamerotics are revered today as an integral component of Italian cinematic history. They perhaps reveal more about their social context than any of the overtly commentative films of Lina Wertmuller or the Taviani brothers, mainly because they don't presume to say anything. But when taken as a catalogue, when the parts are assembled into a whole, the humble presence of the Decamerotics outshines its contemporaries' ivory tower intellectualism, masked either as 'satire' or 'neo-realism', in their treatment of the human condition. If we can learn anything from Pasolini, it is this: that the Joe D'Amatos of the world give more truth for their dollar than Pasolini himself could ever afford.

Kier-La Janisse is the author of *A Violent Professional* and *House of Psychotic Women*.

footnotes

1   Krista Nell was the girlfriend of Ettore Manni, who starred in Fellini's **La città delle donne**, and died of leukaemia shortly after her stint in the Decamerotics. Manni shot himself after Nell passed away.
2   Gabriella Giorgelli remarked in the book *99 Women* that she had reservations about working with Crostarosa, who "came from a noble family and had the fixation of being an actor... he was slim, skinny, so small and graceful among all those matronal maneaters!" (Gomarasca and Pulici, p.253).
3   The Masetto story is predated by Francesco da Barberino's book *Del regimento e costumi di donne* (circa 1309), wherein a group of Spanish nuns are tempted by an incubus named Rasis, who leaves the convent full of impregnated nuns who are later stoned to death for their indiscretions. (Fentone, p.11)
4   Decamerotics based on Aretino's works, or claiming to be, were just as likely as those deriving inspiration from *The Decameron*. For example: **L'Aretino nei suoi ragionamenti** (Enrico Bomba, 1972), **...E si salvò solo l'Aretino Pietro con una mano avanti e l'altra dietro** (Silvio Amadio, 1972), **I giochi proibiti dell'Aretino Pietro** (Piero Regnoli, 1972), and **Le notti peccaminose di Pietro l'Aretino** (Manlio Scarpelli, 1972).
5   A jongleur is a travelling medieval entertainer; Marcabru was an influential 12th Century Spanish jongleur.
6   Alfaro's film was one of many Decamerotics to star Femi Benussi, whose classic looks made her a primary casting choice for these films. "While this genre remained in vogue," writes Erik Sulev in *ETC* #9, "Benussi remained on top." (p.37). It is ironic that Pasolini's indirect influence would be responsible for popularizing her image, since it was Pasolini's **Uccellacci e uccellini** (aka **Hawks and Sparrows**, 1966) that provided Benussi with her breakthrough role.
7   Although a reference to homosexuality in the film's title may be unique, homosexuality itself is no stranger to the Decamerotics. Pasolini's film has Ciapelletto referred to as "a little bit of a fairy" among a list of his various crimes, and Guerrini's **Decameron No. 2** sees a wife's lover seduced by her husband, thus explaining the latter's sexually neglectful behaviour towards her. However, the free circulation of homosexuals in these films depended on the character having obviously 'gay' characteristics, a requirement by the censor board. Even "to attempt Sappho in a Decamerotic film is a stroke of genius as well as a decided infraction of the rules," says Davide Pulici, "which deep down are very prudish and bourgeois..." Pasolini's film has the most overtly homoerotic aesthetic of all the Decamerotic films, which "represents a fantasmatic negotiation of his subjective homosexuality in his particular time and place, an eroticism that is intimately informed by the homophobic consumerist culture in which it developed." (Jill M. Ricketts)

bibliography

Bergin, Thomas Goddard. Boccaccio. New York, NY: Viking Press, 1981. ISBN 9780670177356

Bertolino, Marco and Ridola, Ettore. Vizietti all'italiana: L'epoca d'oro della commedia sexy. Firenze, Italy: Molino, 1999. ISBN 9788890035920

Blumenstock, Peter and Kessler, Christian. "Interview with Alberto De Martino" in European Trash Cinema Volume 2 #11, 1995

Fentone, Steve. AntiCristo: The Bible of Nasty Nun Sinema and Culture. Godalming, Surrey: FAB Press, 2000. ISBN 9781903254035

Ginsborg, Paul. A History of Contemporary Italy: Society and Politics, 1943-1988. London: Penguin, 1990. ISBN: 9780140124965

Gomarasca, Manlio and Pulici, Davide. 99 Donne: Stelle e stelline del cinema Italiano. Milano, Italy: Nocturno Cinema/Media World, 1999.

Greene, Naomi. Pier Paolo Pasolini: Cinema as Heresy. Princeton, NJ: Princeton University Press, 1992. ISBN 9780691000343

Hoyt, Robert S. and Chodorow, Stanley. Europe in the Middle Ages. New York, NY: Harcourt Brace Jovanovich, 1976. ISBN 9780155247123

Liehm, Mira: Passion and Defiance: Film in Italy from 1942 to the Present. Berkeley, CA: University of California Press, 1986. ISBN 9780520057449

Martines, Lauro. Power and Imagination: City-States in Renaissance Italy. New York, NY: Random House, 1979. ISBN 9780394501123

Miles, Margaret R. "Achieving the Christian Body: Visual Incentives to Imitation of Christ in the Christian West" in Hornik, Heidi J. and Parsons, Mikeal Carl (eds.) Interpreting Christian Art. Macon, GA: Mercer University Press, 2003. ISBN 9780865548503

Ricketts, Jill M. Visualizing Boccaccio: Studies on Illustrations of the Decameron, from Giotto to Pasolini. Cambridge: Cambridge University Press, 1997. ISBN 9780521496001

Stearns Schenck, Mary Jane. The Fabliaux: Tales of Wit and Deception. Amsterdam: John Benjamins Publishing Company, 1987. ISBN 9780915027897

Tannahill, Reay. Sex in History. London: Hamish Hamilton, 1980. ISBN 9780241102008

Thompson, N. S. Chaucer, Boccaccio, and the Debate of Love: A Comparative Study of The Decameron and The Canterbury Tales. Oxford: Clarendon Press, 1996. ISBN 9780198123781

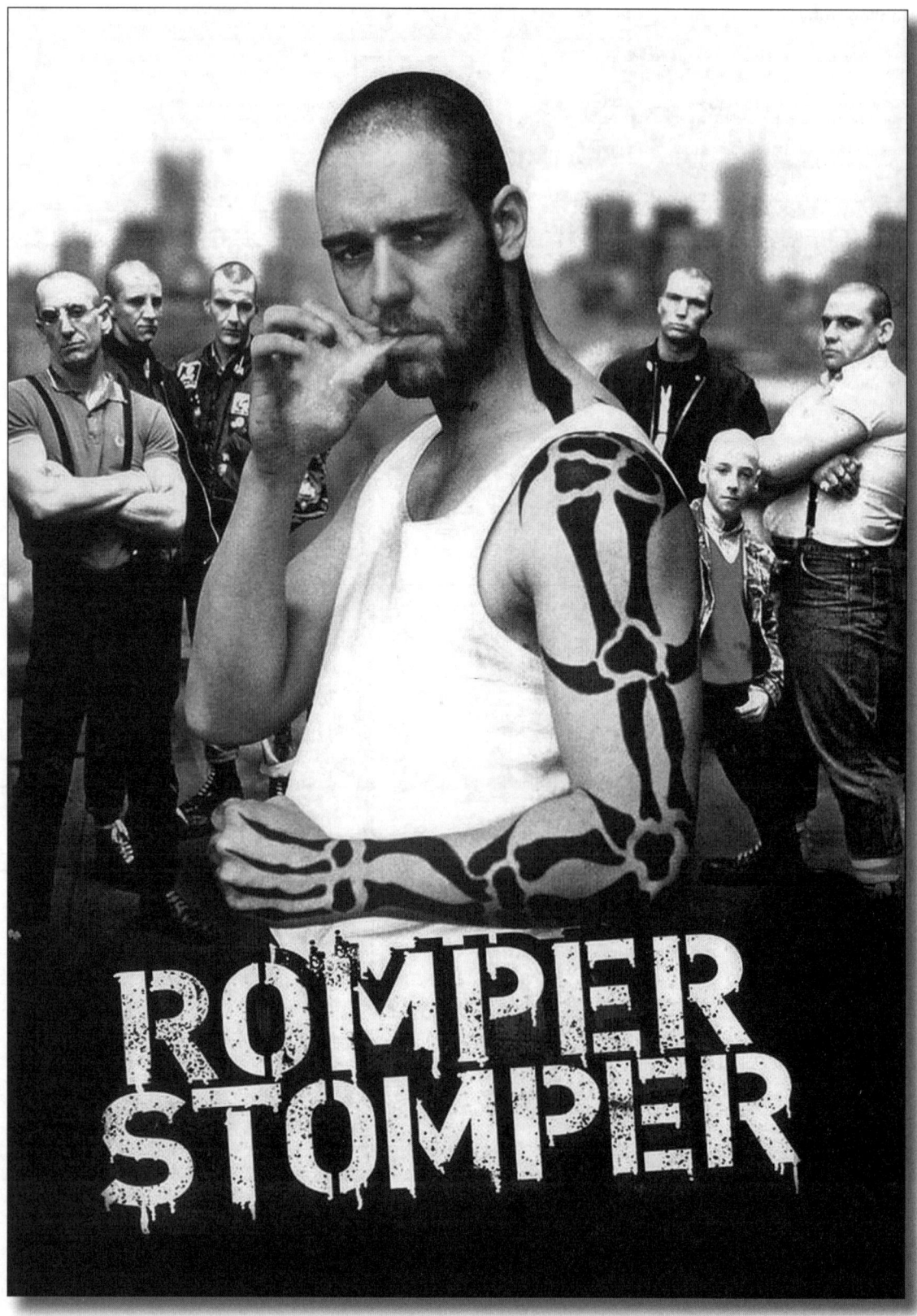

Adrenaline Vision

A Discussion with Australian Filmmaker Geoffrey Wright

Marcus Stiglegger

Australian director Geoffrey Wright is famous for two of the angriest and most kinetic adolescent/counter-culture dramas of recent decades – the neo-Nazi skinhead tragedy **Romper Stomper** and the suburban crash-kid elegy **Metal Skin**. Both films share an absolutely reckless attention to ambivalent characters and a sensitive, almost physical cinematic approach. The following discussion took place in spring 2001, shortly after Wright's Hollywood debut, the darkly ironic teen-slasher flick **Cherry Falls** (2000), had been literally butchered by its American production company to please the preview crowd and the MPAA. Yet still Wright's strong directorial style is very much evident in this beautifully photographed (Anthony Richmond) horror film. Much of what follows is not overly familiar, even to those who enjoyed the extensive interviews with Wright on the **Romper Stomper** and **Metal Skin** DVDs...

Marcus Stiglegger: Please, tell us something about your past as a film critic. What kind of education did you go through? How did the change of profession come about?

Geoffrey Wright: I went to Swinburne film school, so I learned the rudiments of camera and editing and script structure under the guidance of a wonderful man called Brian Robinson, who started the school with Phillip Adams – an advertizing exec and journalist. Brian died in 1992, Mr. Adams still writes for various Australian papers and is very well known. After Swinburne I worked as a truck driver, cleaner, various very odd jobs, then started working for the *Melbourne Age* – a big paper – as a movies-on-TV reviewer, plus Radio 3AW, as a theatrical release reviewer, and the *Melbourne Times* – a smaller, inner city paper – as a theatrical release reviewer. This was a nice way to think about movies – getting paid to watch them! It was a lot of fun, but it's not a very important job and you get restless so I decided I wanted to make movies. Needless to say, when you jump the fence and start making them, your old colleagues back in the critic game can get pretty vengeful. ("Who does he think he is ...?")

*There is a film called **The Club** mentioned in your filmography. What work did you do on it?*

Well, as a teenager I worked on a Bruce Beresford movie called **The Club**. I was a third assistant director, and my boss – the first AD – was the guy that eventually directed **Shine**. I remember being fired toward the end of the shoot after I dropped a three piece plastic funnel into a grip's petrol tank, all very ignominious.

*Your debut feature, **Loverboy**, is not known in Europe. Can you tell us something about this project? Why did you choose it as your debut? How did you manage the difficulties of being a first time director?*

Loverboy was really my first film made for the public; my few things before that being little experimental bits. It starred Noah Taylor [later seen in **Shine** and **Almost Famous**] and Gillian Jones. It's only an hour long – that's all we could shoot for the money. In Australia they released it theatrically with another short feature and the double played quite nicely. Noah, along with Ben Mendelsohn [**Map of the Human Heart**, **Australia**] and Daniel Pollock [**Romper Stomper**] were all in it. They were the best young actors in the country at the time and good friends and I dearly wanted to get all three in a true feature. That never happened; Daniel died after making **Romper Stomper**. **Loverboy** was about a relationship between a 16-year-old male and a woman around 40. I remember at the time being criticised because the ending was unhappy and many commentators felt I was dismissing 'pan generational relationships'. Well, I'm sorry, but these relationships *are* mostly doomed to failure, though not necessarily in the melodramatic way depicted in this little film. My God, you realize it's really endless what you can be criticised for.

Did you have certain idols, influences etc. you could name?

I loved the way Kubrick found a way to have a career that spanned the mainstream yet dealt with very un-Hollywood ideas. **Barry Lyndon**, **Dr. Strangelove**, **A Clockwork Orange**, **Paths of Glory**, **2001: A Space Odyssey**, these are all wonderful movies and we'll never see the like of them again. On a face to face level I remember meeting a certain Italian journalist at several Italian film festivals. Her name was Sandra Bordigoni, she's written many articles and at least one book on Australian films and she encouraged me and inspired me immensely whenever we met. Wonderful commentator and a very positive spirit. She really has been a critically important propagator of Australian film information throughout Europe.

Tell us something about your first steps in the making of **Romper Stomper**. *How did the topic come about? Was there a degree of morbid fascination, researching vandalism and violent subcultures?*

Romper Stomper came about because it was a subject that cropped up in the papers I worked for, either in stories about Australia or Europe. It seemed like a great subject; I was always interested in skinheads because we had them at highschool, you know, but in those days our skinheads were *not* political – just drunks and vandals without any racial ideas, they seemed to hate everyone equally. They looked like the future skinheads but we also, in those days, called them 'sharpies'. Some of them listened to reggae music – which shows you how indifferent to racial notions they were. But I saw the transition to a kind of organized neo-Nazi point of view and found this fascinating. A lot of this transition took place when, across the world, two things seemed to happen: firstly there was a lot of youth unemployment; and secondly there was a lot of immigration. This sort of led to a lot of people looking for someone to blame in Britain, Germany, Australia and other places – like France too, I presume. So Pakistanis were attacked in London, Turks in Germany, Vietnamese in Australia and North Africans in Paris. Of course, the Jews were blamed for the mess in central Europe during the '30s. In times of economic uncertainty minorities get singled out and picked on – in the case of the Jews it led to the concentration camps and mass murder. I wrote a screenplay about the 'new' Australian skinheads, didn't like it and began to research them properly – I still have about 40 hours of taped interviews. **Romper Stomper** is, like most of these things, a mix of several stories that took place over several years. I combined and condensed them so the story took place in a few weeks. I went to the funding bodies but they wanted me to make a short film first – therefore I wrote and made **Loverboy**, which was my ticket to **Romper Stomper**... incidentally, **Metal Skin** was also written before we shot **Romper Stomper**. The funding bodies were nervous about the project but admitted it was a good plot, very tense, and you kept wanting to know what happened. There was a lot of behind the scenes fighting about whether it should be made but the bolder souls carried the day

and it went into production. Of course, everyone now likes to claim that they helped this controversial little movie to get made but I suspect its true friends – at the time – were few in number and their audacity was sorely tested, but more power to them! A woman at the AFC at the time, Lynn Gailey, was very important to us; there were several others, I remain in their debt.

Did you ever have problems with the artistic 'distance'? What about the other staff members?

What people forget about **Romper Stomper** is that one of the two key producers – Daniel Scharf – is Jewish and so were half a dozen other members of the crew. Daniel never had any concerns about the morality of the film, but, you know, I've never heard a complaint from a person of Jewish descent or background or faith. Neither have I heard a complaint from a Vietnamese person. Perhaps it's a generalization but I find Jews and Vietnamese to be immensely practical people of great common sense. They understand, as the film's detractors do not, that it is not only acceptable to make Hando a charismatic leader it is *essential* to the point of the story. That is, that very destructive people are not without attractive traits. Of course, Shakespeare understood this really well, Macbeth, Richard III are very bad people who had admirable courage that could easily match a 'good' man like Henry V. You won't have a convincing Hando unless he has some charm, some attraction, something human about him. I mean, is anyone going to argue that Hitler didn't have compelling public speaking skills or – on a mundane, everyday level – didn't show kindness to his dog (before he poisoned it along with himself and Eva Braun at the bunker). The point is that Hitler was not a being from another world or a supernatural force, he was a *man*, a man with certain skills and a lot of violent emotions and vaulting ambition. As a species we have a tendency to create superstitious myths out of influential people and we forget how much we still have in common with them. However, as it is said, 'there but for the grace of God go we…' I think that the question of objectivity is without meaning to a lot of method actors. In prepartion for his role, Russell Crowe, while never acting in a racist way, certainly started bossing around the other members of the cast. They fell into line very quickly and Russell would lead them on nightly escapades which climaxed in a kind of mass arrest at a hotel in the Melbourne suburb of Toorak – the hotel was a haunt for wealthy, middle class kids and Russell showed up there and, I'm told, challenged the patrons to a fight. Of course, in his skinhead regalia and shaved head he looked a fearsome sight and no one budged – I'm told it was like something out of Sergio Leone movie – you know, those scenes where the bad guy comes

above: Now a worldwide superstar, New Zealander Russell Crowe's first feature film role was the part of violent skinhead Hando in Geoffrey Wright's **Romper Stomper** (1992). Sharon Stone reputedly helped Crowe take a leap up the industry ladder after being so impressed by his performance in Wright's movie that she briefly held up filming of **The Quick and the Dead** until he was free to take up a role in the film, which she co-produced.

into town and terrorizes the locals. Anyway, he yelled a bit and threw furniture around, broke a billiard cue or something and everyone was scared and someone called the cops. Russell and almost the entire cast were then arrested. The producer called me up at about 4am and said that the cast were, "in jail and I'm going to leave them there for a while till they cool off." Russell – of course – did most of the talking to the cops, which led to more trouble. After a while he and the others admitted they were actors and that they were all 'in character'. The cops started laughing and told him he had to think of a better story than that. Nevertheless, his furious insistence made him seem particularly delusional and he was given his own cell while the others remained herded together in threes and fours. Eventually, the producers did get the cast out of jail. Things quietened down after that – for a while at least.

*Did you meet actual neo-Nazis during the making and screening of **Romper Stomper**? What was their reaction, how did you react?*

I did, of course speak to many neo-Nazis before shooting **Romper Stomper**. It wasn't easy at first, everyone was suspicious but most people like being the centre of attention, and they started to open up, to talk, to let me hang out with them – not while they were rampaging of course, but while they were doing everyday things; cooking, shopping, fighting with their girlfriends, getting a little drunk – always a bit risky to be around at that time – and so on. I never lied to them. They knew I had to tell a compelling story and that didn't mean a happy ending for them. While doing the research some of them made the transition out of the gangs and these became the most useful contacts, they told me of their fears, their frustrations, their disillusionment with everything including the neos and the question of… what now? The house, the wife, the husband, the TV and the kids who would be as angry as they were until they ran out of steam… was that life? Some were frightening, filled with hatred and very dangerous. Others were potentially dangerous but much more inclined to follow the lead of others, and, when not led, seemed rather harmless. Some had a past of violence and discontent but for all sorts of reasons – age, injury, a stable relationship, a period of incarceration – had left the gangs and settled down to become fairly average citizens. They were a very mixed bag. What struck you amongst the less anti-social ones was how mundane they were except for this neo thing which was either in the past or supressed in the present, the excesses of youth, as it were. It occured to me, when researching, that very few of them had an interest in real politics, that is, how the world, how nations, are run. What many of them were attracted to was a system of thought, a tribe, that would give them licence to be out of control, to smash things and people, to give vent to rage or the thrill of destruction. *This* was the magnet, like a drug, like adrenaline. The neo thing said it was OK to be out of control, to be anti-social, to be criminal. It was this permissive, very primitive thing which people forget when talking about the rise or bubbling under of these kinds of movements. They appeal to the basest instincts and to kids – this can be exhilarating. In Australia I did meet a bunch of skins after a screening of the film – and I had watched them while the film was on. They started out cheering for Hando at first, but as things went down hill in the fortunes of the gang their reactions were quieter and as the lights went up they were angry or sullen that 'their side' had ended that way. I think most people's reactions to the film are not straightforward; the film delivers a certain adrenaline rush, like a roller coaster, only to end on a 'downer'. There's nothing simple about this and it gets under people's skin. I think **Romper Stomper** is a much better film than **Natural Born Killers**, which really goes absolutely nowhere in its closing scenes. **Romper Stomper** is determined, I think, to throw a spanner in the works of the viewer in a way which political forces, left and right, don't usually want. They want simple messages that tradition has taught them can and should be absorbed by people.

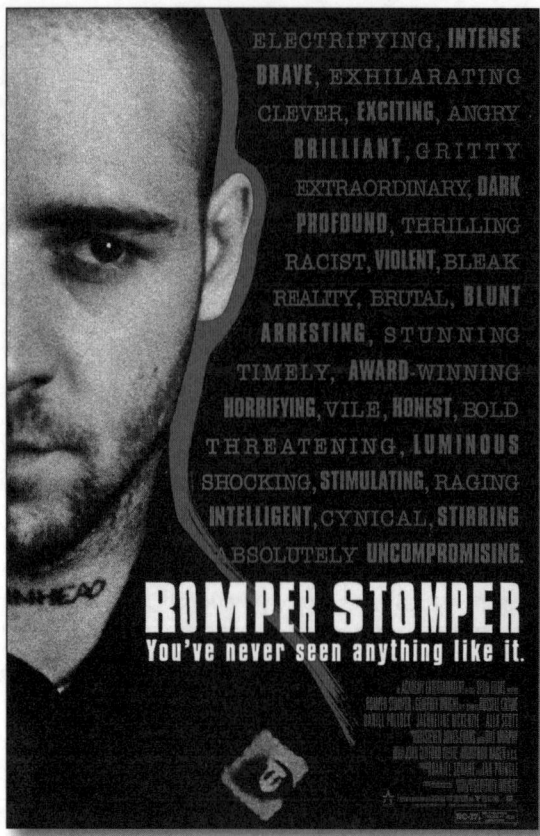

ELECTRIFYING, INTENSE
BRAVE, EXHILARATING
CLEVER, EXCITING, ANGRY
BRILLIANT, GRITTY
EXTRAORDINARY, DARK
PROFOUND, THRILLING
RACIST, VIOLENT, BLEAK
REALITY, BRUTAL, BLUNT
ARRESTING, STUNNING
TIMELY, AWARD-WINNING
HORRIFYING, VILE, HONEST, BOLD
THREATENING, LUMINOUS
SHOCKING, STIMULATING, RAGING
INTELLIGENT, CYNICAL, STIRRING
ABSOLUTELY UNCOMPROMISING.

ROMPER STOMPER
You've never seen anything like it.

The idea of saying, in a creative work, that the appeal of fascism is very much about a licence to act out of control – and making that point on a visceral level that pumps adrenaline for the viewer the same way that the members of the gang pump adrenaline – is just too sophisticated and ambitious a notion for them to come to terms with. They are not equipped for it on a policy level. What the left and right have in common is a fear that the individual cannot think for themselves and must be organized and saved from themselves. The point is, if the viewer gets excited in the chase scene and the skinheads in the movie also got excited in the chase scene – how different are you fundamentally or physiologically? The answer: not very. And there's the rub, that's what drives the detractors of the film crazy. A creative work, to them, should never get this intimate, but remain stand-offish, objective, in the realm of a deep perspective that shows THEM – those evil skinheads from outer space – and US – the good people who would *never* do that and may judge from afar. Huh?! Really? Skinheads are not *that* different from anyone else.

*Did you see **American History X** and **Oi! Warning**? How do you see **Romper Stomper** in relation to them?*

I haven't seen **Oi! Warning** but I did see **American History X** – it's not a bad film at all, wonderful lead.

However, I think the fringe is still the best place to tackle such a hot topic as skinheads because you can be blunt. Hollywood can never entirely escape a certain comfortable perspective.

Did you hear about the outrage and censorship this film suffered in Germany? There are parts of the dialogue erased, and the Japanese tourists are entirely missing. What do you think about this?

I didn't know the Japanese tourist scene is missing from the German version! It never ceases to amaze me how reactionary and superstitious censors can be – and often what they are afraid of varies from territory to territory. The Americans had no problem at all with the Japanese but major problems with some of the party sex. Why cut the Japanese tourists? I defy anyone to debate the logic of that with me. These censorship issues are, to me, 'superstitious' in nature, as if by purging a work of certain images you can 'cleanse' it and 'improve' it. The Japanese were *not* criticised in the original version; their presence merely indicated that in the modern world economic superiority is *everything* and pathetic, useless notions of racial superiority lead to chaos and disaster because racial superiority holds no more truth than saying green is superior to blue, circles to squares – it's entirely senseless. The lost scene was about that, and a point to make to the neo-Nazis who might have seen the film. The modern world is not interested in racial superiority, it responds to money, capital. Apart from anything else, the neo-Nazis are utterly anachronistic in terms of what makes the world turn. The Japanese in the scene had disposable income, they were able to travel the world, they didn't really know what to make of the ludicrous, tragic melodrama that took place in the sand beneath them. The tone of the brief words spoken between them as they look across the beach to the skinheads is hushed, shocked and confused. One can imagine the censor reacting on a primitive level to this juxtopsition of elements, "oh my God, the director is inciting the skinheads with this display of Japanese arrogance, look, they're on a cliff, they're higher up than the skinheads…" Well, yes, they *are* higher up, money makes you higher up, and they are innocent, that helps too. If I might diverge here, and talk about history for a moment, it's not insignificant that the Japanese were, in the war years, a fascist force of their own who worked, not closely with Hitler's Germany, at least in some sort of occasional concert. The grand cooperation planned between the nations – to have their advancing forces link up somewhere in Iran and also in Madagascar – never eventuated. The Japanese have been accused of not facing up to their criminal actions in the war – particularly the attack on Nanking and their experiments on Chinese peasants, which rivalled those of the German concentration camps, however, despite this, no one fears Japan the way parts of the world still fear Germany, and Germany has been more inclined to face up to its past. I wonder why this is? Perhaps because the Japanese are surrounded by many strong or potentially strong neighbours – these days – while Germany appears to be the hub of Europe – still. Furthermore, it's inconceivable that the Japanese youth would ever wear a uniform or sport a haircut advocating the reintroduction of fascist policies. This may have been due to the fact also that the Japanese were not occupied in the same way that East Germany was occupied – I don't know.

Did the allergic reaction of 'anti-fascist' groups ever offend you?

Life is so strange, I am, of course, left wing in my politics, I've always voted for the Australian Labor Party, for example. But being left doesn't mean *not* exploring story and character and reacting to creative choices like a domineering automaton, itself dominated by dogma and panic. I think the most illuminating thing from the release of **Romper Stomper** was the reaction of the Anti Fascist League in London which physically blocked people from going to see the movie by parading outside the door of the theatre with banners, heckling and jostling patrons. Honestly, at that moment the AFL behaved *exactly* like the Brownshirts. And what were they suggesting to the public? See this movie and you'll become a Nazi? Watch out, your brain will be converted by the evil film? What can one say to that except that people are strange. They get scared, they love the power of the mob; that makes them feel like they're accepted and empowered – politics isn't all about political power, sometimes it's about acceptance, family, a licence to act in a way that stimulates excitement and makes you feel you're alive. The correct approach would have been for the AFL to *see* the film – most of them of course didn't – and allow anyone else to see it, then talk about it, talk to me, talk to the people who supported the movie and ask why do they like it? Have they been brain damaged by the experience? Brainwashed? That sort of thing. Had the AFL forgotten that Hitler banned jazz and modern art because it was 'decadent' and for what it might do to people's brains? Can they learn nothing from history? Any political force that seeks to censor to that extent is a force that has lost its higher, nobler instincts and has become the modern day version of the Witchfinder General, burning suspicious individuals to prevent 'evil spells' and crop failure. By acting like complete idiots the AFL handed the local fascists a cheap moral victory. Suddenly the bullying of one side was indistinguishable from that of the other. Such is life.

How did it feel to experience this film again during the DVD commentary?

Doing a commentary like that brings back many memories – sad in this case because Daniel Pollock had died after the shooting of the movie and one was forced to reflect upon the brevity of his life and the tenuousness of life in general, how fragile, how fleeting everything is and how it's important not to waste a single day – every day is a gift. Life is a mystery, it always will be, you have to be humble and accept it as a passing gift, make the most of it and respect it. Watching the film again I was also aware of how good Russell was and how it didn't surprise me that he rose to the heights in Hollywood that he did. What's evident is that talent is always there from the beginning, as his talent is. Jackie McKenzie and I are still good friends, having endured some periods of distance or misunderstanding. She works in the US quite a bit and I do want to work with her again. I'd love to work with Russell too but I might need $20 million to do it! I'm proud that **Romper Stomper** remains one of the best examples of the work of Daniel, Jackie and Russell. The film looks unbearably rough to me now, but placed in the context of the time and the resources it still reveals a surprising amount of energy and it still confronts. It's a fearless little tiger that really earned its stripes against a very large array of adversarial forces.

I always wondered how this Gothic girl came into contact with Hando's clan. Isn't Goth a declared enemy of neo-Nazis?

You mean the two who followed the group around? Anyway, yes, you are quite right about Goths and neos being basically at odds with each other. However, people being what they are, strange connections are often made, officially party policy is overlooked, especially where sex is involved. I wanted to keep my group rough around the edges, not automatons but, in some small ways, very regular, that is to say, taking sex where they can find it. Besides which, if a person from a rival tribe is as destructive and rootless as you are, then, in certain desperate circumstances, you might forget the rules and link up, sleep together and so on. All this seemed to add to the characters' sense of being swept along the streets of life without as much control as they thought they had.

this page: Aden Young stars as 'Psycho Joe' in **Metal Skin**, Wright's epic 1994 study of hotrods, Satanists and disaffected youth living life on the edge.

I often think that there is a strange link between the fervour of the conservationists who sabotage tree loggers or chemical plants and the fervour of ancient cultures who worshipped the forest gods and tore interlopers limb from limb. There is a great passion about the green movement that is not entirely explained by 'direct action' type politics – which, by the way – I entirely sympathize with.

*Metal Skin has – even more so than **Romper Stomper** – very few likeable characters. In fact these racing-youths show either physical or internal 'ugliness'. This is remarkable for a film that's aimed at a young audience looking for role-models, etc. The anti-soap approach. Would you agree? How did the Australian audience respond to **Metal Skin**?*

*The Gothic element is actually a link between **Romper Stomper** and **Metal Skin**. Are you particularly interested in these subculture and their connection to pagan and occult groups?*

Well, paganism is a colourful element in film, literally. It amazes me where it crops up. Even in Hollywood you'd be surprised – or perhaps you wouldn't – at the number of 'nature worshipers' you find here, you know, spells, white magic, that sort of thing. I think its role in Western history has been a little underrated in view of the official line of Christianity. But of course Christianity, particularly Catholic Christianity, built its foundations by meshing with the remains of paganism. All the big Christian holidays fall on important pagan dates and a kind of kid culture with Easter rabbits, Father Christmas and so on, has been allowed to continue its existence on a very open basis. The names of the months, the names of the weekdays, and the astrological columns in every magazine and paper, all bear witness to a pagan tradition that is still alive. You may even see a further revival of it in the form of the green movement.

I will say this about **Metal Skin** – I thought we really were onto something about the nature of the explosive anger that leads to 'senseless killings' as headlined in newspapers, you know, 'a man killed his three children and then shot himself…' That kind of domestic nightmare tragedy. **Metal Skin** got a very hostile reaction from critics and the audience. The critics had already attacked **Romper Stomper** and got a little burnt by the surprising support that the audience showed for it by seeing it in good numbers. **Metal Skin** never had that kind of protection. It's an extremely 'difficult' piece, no easy access, no identifiable hero or Satanic anti-hero, like the criminal Hando. Everyone loses. My God, it's such a downer. I saw it on the big screen a couple of years back and was shocked at how dismal and cruel the film is. Oh well, I did it and have to stand by it but I was shocked at myself, I wonder what I was thinking? I guess it was a journey into the dark heart of something in my head and I respect the guy who made it for going through to the bitter end but there was *never* any chance of the film developing a following; it's just too objective, too dark. The Canadian fringe press called it 'the angriest film ever made'. Some elements of the press at home have looked at it again some years after its release; no revision here but there is the notion that I was trying something unusual and it isn't simply 'appalling' as many commentators claimed at the time. Personally, I find the film frightening, immensely disturbing because of what we did with the soundtrack which is, I think, a very complex one. Frank Lipson, who designed the sound, still remarks on it. **Metal Skin** remains a strange, disquietening enigma even to me. I don't ever want to see it again, it really fucks with the nervous sytem on a physiological level when you play it through big speakers. On a mundane note I have to say that what we did with that final car chase on 3 million Australian dollars was pretty amazing.

You seem to be very interested in coming of age topics and youth counterculture?

I don't pursue coming of age projects these days, but they still find me. I may end up doing another one but I really don't have any special interest in that genre. Unfortunately, what I would really love to do is examine a very particular European historical figure, every chapter of his life winds up being a movie in itself, the more research I do the more astonished I become. There's no doubt in my mind that he's the most interesting man since the apostles Peter and Paul. His whole life seems like some blatant morality tale, he appears to have been a literary creation and certainly to some extent he is, but the truth – or at least the observations of others about him – seem even more fascinating. I don't want to say who it is, I'm afraid that Hollywood will get hold of the idea and really screw it up. Meanwhile, I remain as busy as a bee doing my homework, and perhaps one day…

Have you ever directly dealt with autobiographical elements in your films so far?

No, my films are not autobiographical at all, except that, as a youth, I certainly understood boredom and frustration – I guess most of us do.

*Please tell us about the censorship history of **Cherry Falls** from your point of view. What fell under the censor's scissor was mainly the sexual content, wasn't it?*

Yes, what you see in the current release of **Cherry Falls** hangs on to maybe 10% of the original sexual content, not merely for the big 'orgy' scene at the end but particularly between the two leads. When we previewed the uncut **Cherry Falls** in Pasadena we had some very graphic, well acted, discreetly shot love scenes between the two central characters. Well, when these scenes appeared I thought there was going to be a riot in the theatre. The producers turned and looked at me with fear and anger. I wasn't too phased, after all, I been heckled and abused and even threatened after **Romper Stomper** and **Metal Skin**; I was used to it, they were not. We cut those scenes out, it seemed that the kids didn't want to be confronted with that kind of sexuality and they wanted more shocks and blood. That was easy to rectify but the problem was the censor wouldn't let us do it. The censors were reacting to the Columbine massacre, which was in the papers at the time, and felt that our characters were very young and that we would be screwing with the minds of the audience if we went down that path. So, we couldn't add horror, and we had to reduce sex – which of course the censor was even more concerned about. I remember dealing with them after they kept telling us to cut back more and more on the orgy scene till there was really nothing left. We got down to close-ups revealing bare shoulders and kissing faces – there was still a problem because the censor claimed that you could tell there was still movement between the bodies! Yes, I'm sure there was movement between the bodies, there usually is in sexual activity. Anyway, it all had to go.

Especially in your early films you have very elaborate and sensitive erotic moments. How do you work with the actors in those scenes? Do they bring in a lot of their own experiences or do you work out a 'choreography'?

It wasn't hard to shoot. Sex in movies is never hard to shoot. Most actors, even extras, quickly lose inhibitions once you convince them that you – as an individual – are not present as a pervert or voyeur, but as a person trying to tell a story with pictures and that sex has a context within a framework of many other elements – which in all my films it has had. And, you really are *not* there as a voyeur; I'm so busy trying to get the shot, make sure the thing is lit right, keeping the unit moving, keeping to schedule and watching that everyone stays in character that I simply don't have time to get aroused by all this activity even if I wanted to. But spectator sport is not my thing, anyway… Once an actor knows you are there as a professional with professional concerns, serious concerns with their craft, they'll do anything for you, actors are so grateful for a director who has a vision, makes an effort, is worried about the details of their characterization and the consistency of it. My problem is never getting things in the can, it's getting permission to show it. Anyway, back to **Cherry Falls**, we had a horror film that was also a kind of sexual parody, but we had to remove the horror and the sex, so, what's left…? I mean the

daughters of these people that volunteered in masses for the orgy scene – we even got some relatives of some very well known Christian politicians on our list but the producers thought that by getting the son or daughter of a famous Bible basher that we were asking for trouble. As it is there are still some very interesting people appearing that film – interesting because of their connections to some very famous American families. Names were changed in the credits. I also remember many of the conservative local Baptists who we dealt with for various reasons in pre-production cruising the wrap party with all the zeal of the most avid party animal imaginable. Such is the complexity of middle America.

Do you see the chance for a director's cut?

There will never be a director's cut of **Cherry Falls** released. That would cost money that USA simply doesn't want to spend on the movie. You have to understand, when we went into pre-production on **Cherry Falls** the executive who green-lit the project at October Films, where the film had been set up, left the company and it was purchased by USA, who really didn't have any execs who had anything to gain from the movie – after all, it wasn't their idea, so it was safer to do as little for it as possible and hope that it could make some money on cable. You have to understand the executive mentality here; if **Cherry Falls** had done well then the ousted exec would get all the credit, there was absolutely *no* reason for the USA people to stand by the movie, no gain for them you see, only risk. Once our man from October had left, I knew we were going to be ignored. The so-called 'uncensored cut' of the film puts back a couple of harmless shots that you won't even notice. Unfortunately, it's not a real bold step, I don't know why they bothered except that it gives the marketing people a chance to say 'uncut'. But it won't be what you think.

Any last words?

Sorry I went on and on, I didn't mean to but it was good therapy to unearth and express all that personal history – troubled as it has been. Most of it I have not talked about before. I've had fun remembering.

Thanks a lot! We hope to be able to experience your unique cinematic vision again in the near future…

film is a joke, it's obvious the idea of an orgy to protect yourself against a virgin killer is inherently absurd. I feel a little sorry for anyone who doesn't grasp that idea pretty quickly and who attacks the film as some sort of serious work. I mean, come on! In retrospect it was not a good idea to make the film because horror audiences – like most vodka drinkers – want their favourite label *straight*, not blended, especially not blended with elements that we had to mostly cut back on anyway. They will, however, accept a blatant parody, like **Scary Movie**, which is really a series of TV-like sketches in a kind of **Airplain!** tradition – the US audiences *loved* that movie but it really is in the traditional genre of physical comedy and extreme farce. Still, I did have some fun making **Cherry Falls**, I remember one night we couldn't leave the school where we were shooting, I asked the AD's what was going on, why are we all trapped in the school? They said that the local townspeople had heard we were making a sexually lurid vampire movie and in the best tradition of the South had organized a mob of people to keep us bailed up inside and yell at us – and harrass the poor headmaster who had given us permission. Somehow the crowd dispersed and we all got home but I couldn't help laughing about it. Of course it was the sons and

Geoffrey Wright's Feature Films as Director:
Lover Boy (1988)
Romper Stomper (1992)
Metal Skin (1994) aka **Speed**
Cherry Falls (2000)
Macbeth (2006)

this page: Brittany Murphy stars in Wright's typically confrontational **Cherry Falls**, which was somewhat blunted by the curse of big studio compromise.

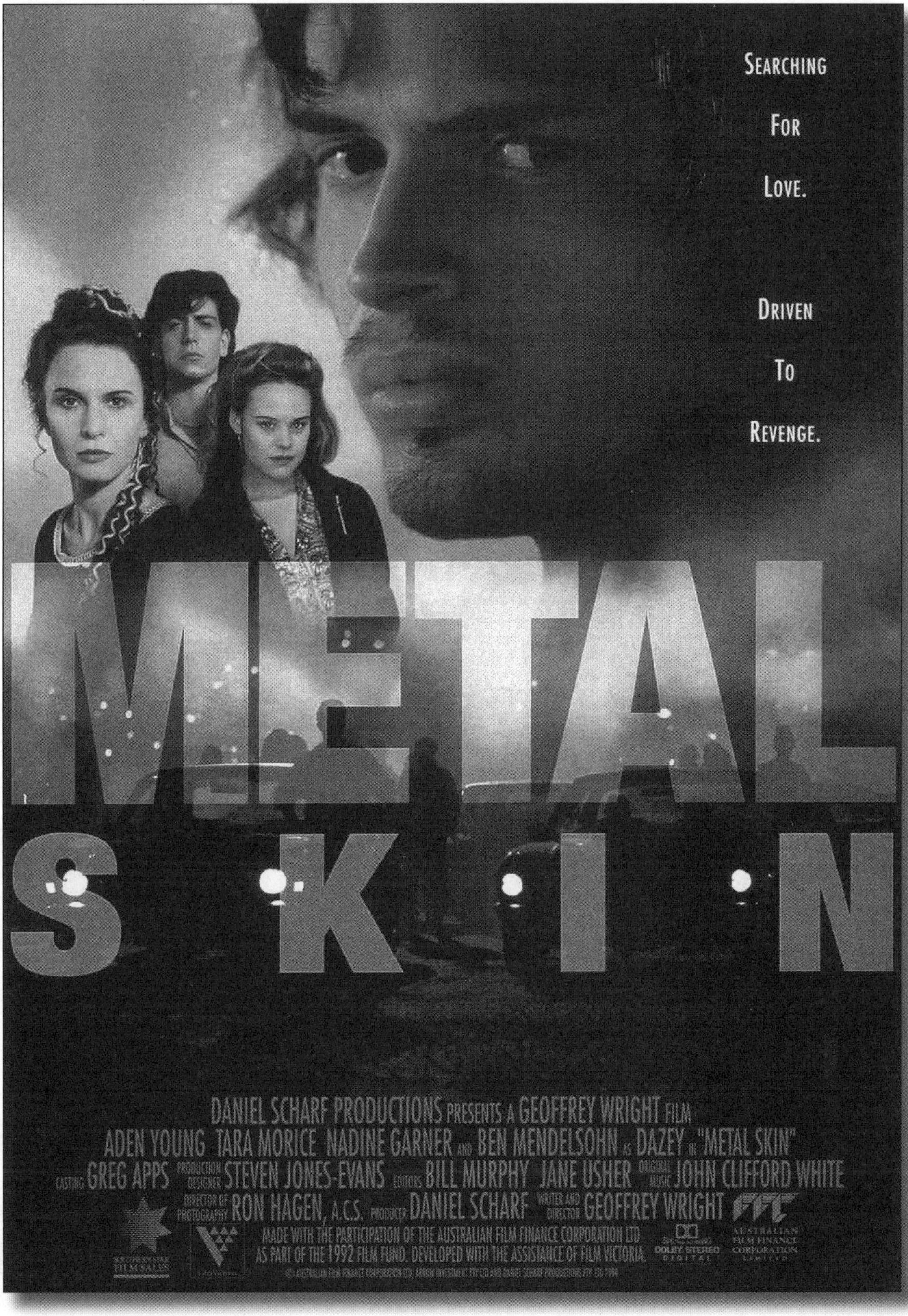

SEARCHING
FOR
LOVE.

DRIVEN
TO
REVENGE.

METAL SKIN

DANIEL SCHARF PRODUCTIONS PRESENTS A GEOFFREY WRIGHT FILM
ADEN YOUNG TARA MORICE NADINE GARNER AND BEN MENDELSOHN AS DAZEY IN "METAL SKIN"
CASTING GREG APPS PRODUCTION DESIGNER STEVEN JONES-EVANS EDITORS BILL MURPHY JANE USHER ORIGINAL MUSIC JOHN CLIFFORD WHITE
DIRECTOR OF PHOTOGRAPHY RON HAGEN A.C.S. PRODUCER DANIEL SCHARF WRITER AND DIRECTOR GEOFFREY WRIGHT

MADE WITH THE PARTICIPATION OF THE AUSTRALIAN FILM FINANCE CORPORATION LTD
AS PART OF THE 1992 FILM FUND. DEVELOPED WITH THE ASSISTANCE OF FILM VICTORIA.
© AUSTRALIAN FILM FINANCE CORPORATION LTD, ARROW INVESTMENT PTY LTD AND DANIEL SCHARF PRODUCTIONS PTY LTD 1994

DOLBY STEREO DIGITAL

SOUTHERN STAR FILM SALES

AUSTRALIAN FILM FINANCE CORPORATION LIMITED

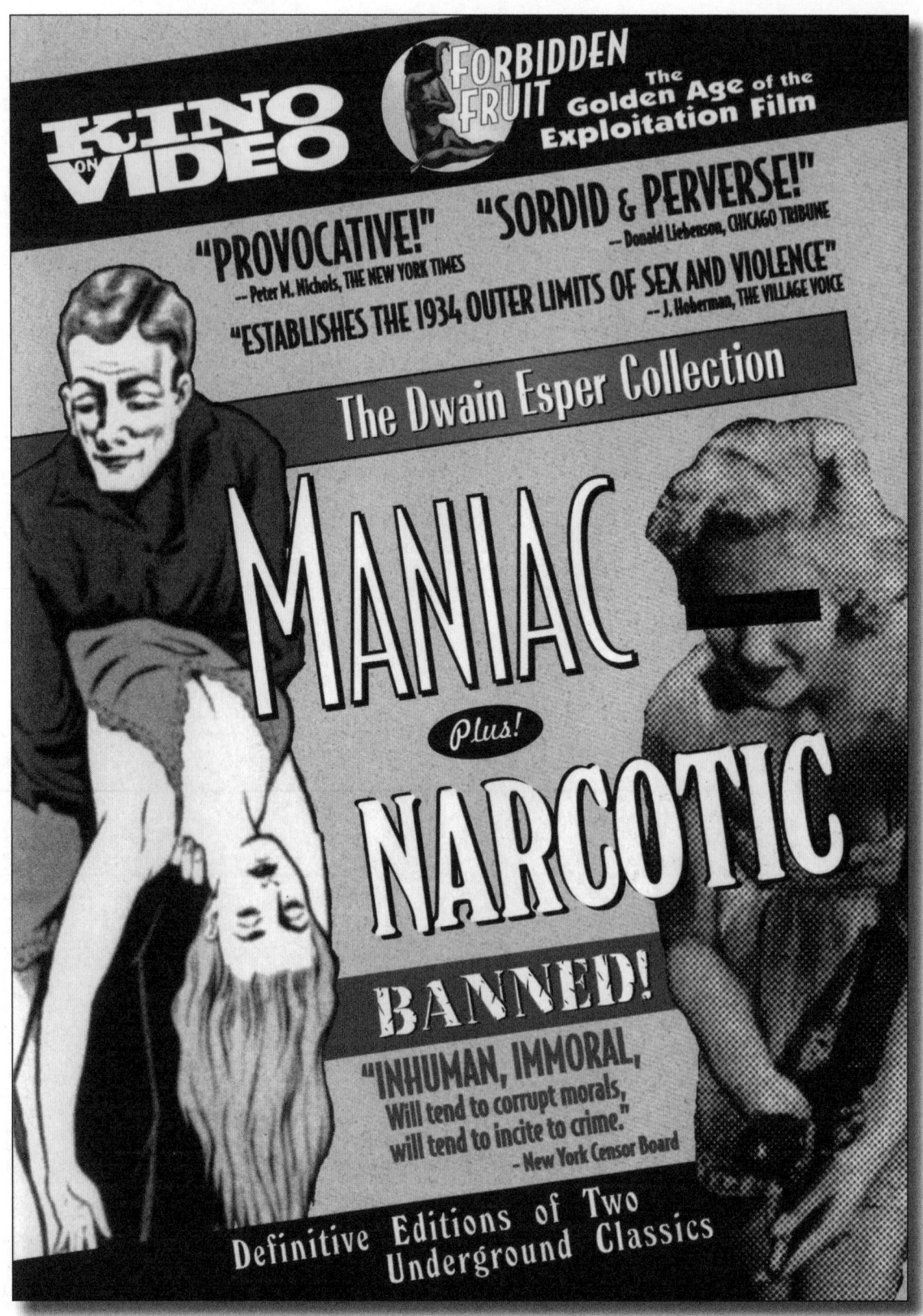

Prince of Exploitation

The Films of Dwain Esper

Robert G. Weiner

The early pioneers of exploitation/sensational motion pictures are the real fathers of the modern independent film. These filmmakers were fundamentally out to make a buck and most cared very little whether their films were technically or artistically any good. Their Do-It-Yourself filmmaking ethic influenced many later filmmakers, not all of whom entered the exploitation arena. They knew how to grab the public's attention through their travelling road shows, lurid advertisements, and use of promoters who would personally travel from town to town with the films. Using the lure of sex, drugs, implied bestiality, nudity, social diseases (VD), sex hygiene, atrocities, crime, abortion, childbirth, eugenics, and violence, exploiters lured audiences – women and men alike – to come and see shows which explored these "forbidden" topics. Some of these movies consisted of documentary medical or anthropological footage spliced into another film in an attempt to make some sort of coherent finished product. A brief consideration of some of the titles shows how this exhibition technique worked to bring part the masses from their money: **Reefer Madness**, **Primitive Passion**, **No Greater Sin**, **Nudist Recruits**, **Naughty in New Orleans**, **Mystery of Birth**, **I Married a Savage**, **Sex Maniac**, **Damaged Goods**, and **Highway to Hell**. Exploitation films were marked more often than not by what they didn't actually show than by what the audience "might" see. By today's standards many of these films are quite tame, but they are no less interesting for it.

No director/producer/distributor deserves to be canonized as one of the greatest in the genre more than Dwain Esper (1893–1982). In a partnership similar to that of German director Fritz Lang and Thea von Harbou, Esper and his wife Hildegarde worked together to promote their distinctive brand of movies. Hildegarde wrote the scripts, while Dwain either produced or directed the features. Esper's role as a promoter of these films cannot be understated. While certainly he did not try to make high art, Esper was the king of turning a profit on exploitation and B-movies. Even though he actually directed, and was involved in making, only a handful of films, Esper's work exemplifies sensationalism at its best and most profitable.

Esper and his wife worked very hard at trying to turn a buck by promoting their movies at theatre grindhouses as an event, not unlike a carnival; fittingly, Esper named one of his companies Roadshow Attractions. His skill at marketing his movies, and indeed himself, are the stuff business student dreams are made of. Before commencing the promotion of his films like **Modern Motherhood**, **Narcotic**, **Marihuana**, and **Maniac**, he had prepared ready-made press stories, which ran in big city as well as small town newspapers. He prepared extravangant displays for his productions, virtually covering theatre entrances in order to ensure that even casual passers-by would be impressed. In fact, looking over a touring itinerary for **Marihuana** throughout Texas one finds that in addition to playing in major cities like Dallas and Austin, as expected, the movie also secured play-dates in smaller, provincial places such as Ballinger, Marfa, and Comanche. Even when sending these films to small towns, Dwain Esper knew how to turn a profit.[1]

The Espers employed lecturers in support of their films to give them the illusion of an educational experience. In common with most early exploitation picture producers, Esper dit not submit his movies to the motion picture code administrators. Esper himself had nothing but disdain for the code and tried to best them in any way he could. Even when he felt it was for the best to be seen to agree to cuts or changes in his films in order to conform to the code, he very rarely actually made those cuts, and proceeded to show the film the way he wanted to anyway. Despite the plethora of loopholes, many early exploitation pictures were wisely presented as morality plays, Esper's movies included.

Esper was above all aggressively money hungry, so much so that film producer Dave Friedman, in an interview with Esper expert Bret Wood, claimed that at one point Esper took to answering the phone with, "I'll sue."[2] He was always involved in a lawsuit of some kind. It's been speculated that Dwain Esper didn't even really like movies. I would not dispute this claim; I would however point out that Esper's films do have a certain charm, despite the bad scripts and poor acting. One might argue that Esper was the Ed Wood of the thirties and forties, but closer examination of his work reveals that this claim is not really fair; there

are certain similarities in editing, style, and the non-actors typically employed, but Wood's films have a serious intent that Esper's don't. Wood always believed in his heart that he was an earnest filmmaker; Esper had no such illusions. For him films were about making money, and if people enjoyed them so much the better for his wallet. With the benefit of hindsight, one now gets the sense from watching Esper's movies or reading the scripts that he knew he was putting one over on the unsuspecting movie-going public.

Esper's first feature movie, **The 7th Commandment** (1932) was a torrid tale of the evils of adultery featuring documentary footage of a Caesarian birth and drama depicting transvestites, bodies infected with syphilis, and nudity. Even though the ultimate message was one of staying faithful to one's partner, a high-ranking official in the Production Code Administration found the film "vile and disgusting".[3] Esper's other marriage morality film, **Modern Motherhood** (1934) tells the story of a newly married couple who want to be free to live their life together without children. They can enjoy the pleasure of each other's bodies without the burden and cost of parenthood. As one would expect, however, the wife does get pregnant and they both realize that mature adults are supposed to be parents. The ultimate message being that if you are married, you should be parents. Unfortunately, a surviving print of either film has yet to be found.

Three of Esper's feature films have been released on DVD: **Marihuana: Weed with Roots in Hell** (1936), **Narcotic** (1933), and **Maniac** (1934). The prints are far from pristine, and the sound is technically primitive, making the dialogue sometimes hard to hear, but at least now, thanks to DVD, the films have been digitized and will therefore be preserved indefinitely for future generations.

Marihuana: Weed with Roots in Hell and **Narcotic** both tell of the evils of drugs and how so many innocent people have been led down the road to death and destruction through their drug addiction. Like many similar exploitation pictures, both of these movies pretend to have been based on real life cases, with law enforcement officials involved.

Marihuana introduces a young, rich girl (Burma) and her friends, who go to a party hosted by a mobster (Tony) and end up smoking this new "giggle weed". Burma gets pregnant at this party by her boyfriend, who also smoked the weed, hence implying that smoking the hellish weed causes people to become morally lax. The kids find themselves in over their heads when one of them commits suicide in the ocean and they are told to keep their mouths shut. Burma's boyfriend ends up drug trafficking for Tony, only to be killed by the police. She gives her baby up for adoption (unknowingly, to her sister) and also starts pushing for Tony. Soon they are both making a lot of money by introducing people to the weed; Burma is then able to get her acquaintances hooked on stronger narcotics, cocaine and heroin. Burma kidnaps her sister's child for a ransom of $50,000 only to find out she is actually its mother. The police raid Tony's apartment, and Burma ends up committing suicide by overdosing on narcotics. The simple moral of the story is that by smoking the "giggle weed" you will most definitely soon try, and then become hooked on, the harder stuff.

Narcotic, a film "interpreted by Dwain Esper", tells the torrid tale of a prominent surgeon, Dr. Davis, who becomes addicted to opium and then moves on to other drugs. He gives up his brilliant career for the sake of drugs and becomes a carnival medicine man selling his product through showmanship, which, of course, is shunned by the traditional medical profession. Ironically, his Chinese friend (Gee Woo), who introduced Davis to the "diversion" of opium, later accompanies the doctor's wife on a visit to a federal narcotics agent to try and understand, and help Davis become free from, the deadly diversion. Woo has the best line in the movie, when he points out that opium smoking for the Chinese is simply an amusement, but for Westerners this amusement becomes a vice. After a bizarre party sequence, Dr. Davis is shown to be at the end of his rope. He is completely lost in his addiction, dishevelled and with a crazed look in his eye. Davis has alienated all of his friends and his family. When he realizes just how far he has fallen, he kills himself by putting a bullet into his head.

Esper's wife, Hildegarde, actually had first hand knowledge of how opium affects people, because her uncle was an addict.[4] As part of the Espers' showmanship expertise, at various screenings of Marihuana and Narcotic they put together displays of sugar, salt, and flour, which they labelled as cocaine, heroin, and opium. So believable were these displays that the FBI came and took them away.[5]

Both films creep at a snail's pace at times and are hopelessly out of touch with reality, but in the realm of exploitation cinema they remain important historical curiosities. They moralize about the evils of drug addiction and use fake newspaper headlines and slogans like, "you can take it out of the body, but not the mind." They pretend to show the viewer what goes on behind closed doors at these drug-crazed parties, where girls take off their clothes and men become bumbling idiots, but in both films the party sequences are so poorly acted, it's comical.

Esper also distributed the short drug documentary **Sinister Menace**, documenting the Egyptian narcotics trade, and the most famous drug film of its time, **Reefer Madness**, but his masterpiece is **Maniac** (later re-titled **Sex Maniac** even though there is very little sex in the film). Made for a little over $7,000, Esper directed and his wife wrote the story. To the average viewer this film is an unmitigated mess, with poor editing, overacting, and a nonsensical narrative. **Maniac** is based very loosely on Edgar Allan Poe's short story *The Black Cat*, with influences drawn from mad scientist stories and films, with Mary Shelley's ubiquitous *Frankenstein* thrown into the mix. In parts, **Maniac** now seems to have more in common with **Re-Animator** than with Universal's **Frankenstein**. Esper presented this film as a case study in psychosis, where the line between fact and fantasy is crossed. The intertitles shown throughout the film discuss how the criminal mind is actually suffering from a mental disease. Esper used statements from a prominent doctor to describe what happens to the brain when fear becomes a "psychic disease". Other mental conditions defined include Dementia praecox; Paresis; Paranoiac; Manic-Depressive Psychosis; and Mania.

Even though Esper presented **Maniac** as a scientific study of dementia, it is really a horror film. The story revolves around a scientist (Dr. Meirschultz) who is researching the possibility of re-animating the dead with his assistant (Don Maxwell). Maxwell is a vaudeville actor on the run from the law whose trade is impersonation. We never find out exactly why the law wants him. Meirschultz manages to keep a heart alive in some

this page and next:
Crazed behaviour in Esper's exploitation classic, **Maniac**.

serum (perhaps foreshadowing films such as **The Brain That Wouldn't Die** and **Donovan's Brain**). Meirschultz and Maxwell steal the body of a woman, who supposedly recently committed suicide, from the morgue... even though it appears that the woman is actually still alive but suffering from some sort of somnambulistic aliment. Meirschultz, not being content with their grave robbing, wants Maxwell to shoot himself so that he can re-animate him. In one of the stupidest scenes in motion picture history Meirschultz gives Maxwell his gun to shoot himself, but instead Maxwell shoots Meirschultz and dons make-up to disguise himself as the scientist. In another nod to Poe, one of the

doctor's patients, Mr. Buckley , thinks of himself as the orangutan from *Murders in the Rue Morgue*. Mrs. Buckley brings him in for a check up and Maxwell accidentally injects him with adrenaline; Buckley goes into a berserk

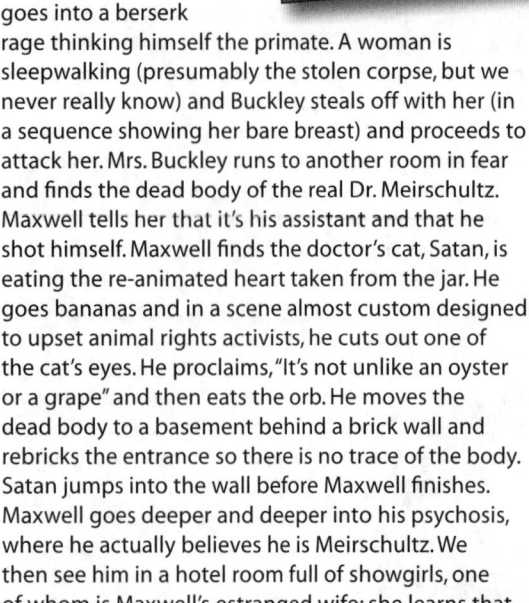

rage thinking himself the primate. A woman is sleepwalking (presumably the stolen corpse, but we never really know) and Buckley steals off with her (in a sequence showing her bare breast) and proceeds to attack her. Mrs. Buckley runs to another room in fear and finds the dead body of the real Dr. Meirschultz. Maxwell tells her that it's his assistant and that he shot himself. Maxwell finds the doctor's cat, Satan, is eating the re-animated heart taken from the jar. He goes bananas and in a scene almost custom designed to upset animal rights activists, he cuts out one of the cat's eyes. He proclaims, "It's not unlike an oyster or a grape" and then eats the orb. He moves the dead body to a basement behind a brick wall and rebricks the entrance so there is no trace of the body. Satan jumps into the wall before Maxwell finishes. Maxwell goes deeper and deeper into his psychosis, where he actually believes he is Meirschultz. We then see him in a hotel room full of showgirls, one of whom is Maxwell's estranged wife; she learns that he has come into a very large inheritance. This scene was obviously thrown in to show some tantalizing, scantily clad cheesecake. Maxwell's wife decides she wants in on the financial action and seeks out her husband. She tells Maxwell, as Meirschultz, the story of the inheritance. Maxwell feels that she is out to kill him because of the "gleam in her eye".

He also feels the same way about Mrs. Buckley. Acting on a tip from the coroner, the police investigate Dr. Meirschultz. The officer comes across one of Meirschultz's neighbours, who complains about his cats being stolen by the doctor for experiments. The neighbour, 'Goof', has a cat farm, in which he raises the animals for their fur. In another scene that would give cat lovers a heart attack, Goof states: "I figured out that the rats breed faster than cats – cats skins make good fur – the cats eats rats. Rats eat raw meat. That is, they eat the carcasses of the cats. So – the cats eat the rats – the rats eat the cats. And I get the skins…" The character of Goof is not credited so he may have actually been a real cat fur farmer that Esper just threw into the story. Bret Wood hypothesizes: "Then the realization hits. The cat coop is no mere prop. It is no mere joke. It is quite real. The Goof's caricature of a demented furrier does not conceal the reality behind the ruse: that some Los Angeles goof was actually breeding and slaughtering cats in his or her backyard for a little extra Depression-era income."**6** When the police finally do break into Meirschultz's lab, they find that Maxwell has locked both Mrs. Buckley and his wife into the basement. They are trying to kill each other because Maxwell has told each of them that the other is insane. Early in the film, Esper showed cats chasing and eating mice, and fighting between dogs and cats. This foreshadows the human catfight coming at the end of the film. (Esper often included footage of animals fighting in his films; for what purpose is anybody's guess). As Mrs. Buckley and Maxwell's wife are fighting a frog jumps between them. The police break down the door of the basement after hearing the screaming and try to stop the fight. Satan screeches from behind the bricks and the authorities find the dead body of Dr. Meirshultz. Maxwell is arrested and put behind bars, proclaiming that all he ever wanted to do was "amuse" and "entertain" and that nobody appreciated his greatest role of Meirschultz.

There are only four major similarities between Poe's story *The Black Cat* and **Maniac**. In both stories

the protagonist goes through a psychosis yet believes he is sane. They both cut out the eye of a cat. They murder someone and try to hide their victim behind a brick wall. When the authorities come to investigate and hear the screeching of the cat behind the wall, they find the body. In Poe's story, the narrator murders his wife and becomes an animal abuser. His dementia revolves around a black cat, which he kills, and then somehow he perceives it coming back to life to haunt him. The cat in the Poe story is named Pluto while Esper's cat is Satan, signifying that the cats represent metaphors for the Lord of the Underworld. Both characters end up in prison.

After repeated viewings, I've come to the conclusion that **Maniac** (while an exploitation picture) also belongs to the class of *avant garde* independent filmmaking in the same class as Lynch's **Eraserhead**, Gilliam's **Brazil**, Russell's **The Lair of the White Worm**, Greenaway's **The Baby of Mâcon**, Svankmajer's **Conspirators of Pleasure**, and anything by Guy Maddin. Even by today's standards, **Maniac** is a bizarre movie. If Dwain Esper had only made **Maniac** and done nothing else, his place in film history would be secure.

footnotes

1 Felicia Feaster, and Bret Wood. *Forbidden Fruit: The Golden Age of the Exploitation Film.* Baltimore, Md: Midnight Marquee Press, 1999. pp.122-123.
2 Bret Wood, ed., *Marihuana, Motherhood, & Madness: Three Screenplays from the Cinema of Dwain Esper.* Lanham, Md: Scarecrow Press, 1998. p.xiv
3 Ibid p.xvii
4 Eric Schaefer. *Bold, Daring, Shocking, True: A History of Exploitation Film 1919-1959.* London: Duke University Press, 1999. p.231.
5 Feaster and Wood. p.149.
6 Wood. p.x.

Films by Dwain Esper on DVD.

Maniac/Narcotic. Both on one DVD from Kino International as the Dwain Esper Collection. DVD extras include trailers, commentary by Esper expert Bret Wood, and footage from the silent movie **Maciste in Hell**, demonstraing which sections are superimposed in **Maniac** to show Maxwell's growing dementia.

Marihuana/Assassin of Youth/Reefer Madness. All three features on one DVD from Something Weird Video, which is advertised as a Triple THC Feature. Extras include the Esper distributed short, **Sinister Menace**, about the Egyptian drug trade, along with several other shorts and trailers.

Selected Filmography:

Films directed by Dwain Esper
> The Seventh Commandment (1932)
> Narcotic (1933)
> Modern Motherhood (1934)
> Maniac (Sex Maniac) (1934)
> Marihuana: Weed with Roots in Hell (1936)
> How to Undress: How to Undress in Front of Your Husband (1937)
> (a 14 min short).

Stock footage compilation films
> Curse of the Ubangi (1934)
> Sinister Menace: Dope Dens of the Orient/The Narcotic Story
> (short film, 8 minutes, usually shown before Esper features).
> March of Crime (1937)
> Expose of the Nudist Racket (1938).
> Hitler's Strange Love Life/Conform or Die/Love of Adolph Hitler (1948)
> Mussolini Speaks (1948)

A representative selection of films owned and distributed by Dwain Esper
> Hollywood Chiselers/Playthings of Hollywood (1930)
> Freaks/Forbidden Love/Nature's Mistakes (1932)
> Bo-Ru the Ape Boy (1934)
> Man's Way with Women (1934)
> Ankgor/Forbidden Adventure/Beyond Shanghai (1935)
> Reefer Madness/Tell Your Children/Love Madness/The Burning Question (1936)
> How to Take a Bath (1937)
> Smashing the Vice Trust (1937)
> No Greater Sin (1939)
> Horrors of War (1940)
> Cannibal Girl/Cain/Rama the Cannibal Girl/Savage Bride (1942, adapted from the 1930 French film Caïn, aventures des mers exotiques.)
> Peep Show (1950)
> Nude Ranch (1951)
> Half Way to Hell/Blood Brothers/The Strange Life and Death of Joseph Stalin (1953)

Selected Bibliography:
Dwain Esper and Exploitation Cinema

Feaster, Felicia, and Wood, Bret. *Forbidden Fruit: The Golden Age of the Exploitation Film.* Baltimore, Md: Midnight Marquee Press, 1999. ISBN: 9781887664240.
A highly readable survey of exploitation filmmaking from its roots in silent film through the 1950s. Includes reproductions of original posters, ad-mats, and film stills. There is a plenty of discussion of how these films were made and promoted.

Landis, Bill and Clifford, Michelle. *Sleazoid Express: A Mind Twisting Tour Through the Grindhouse Cinema of Times Square.* London: Simon and Schuster, 2002. ISBN: 9780743215831.
A heavily illustrated guide to exploitation cinema in New York. Chapters include Mondo Movies, Andy Milligan, Blood Horror, and Celebrity Crime, among others.

McCarty, John, ed., *The Sleaze Merchants: Adventures in Exploitation Filmmaking.* New York, NY: St. Martins Press, 1995. ISBN: 9780312118938.
Interviews with key filmmakers including Ted V. Mikels, David F. Friedman, Herschell Gordon Lewis and Fred Olen Ray. There are chapters on Ed Wood, Jess Franco, Andy Milligan, and Al Adamson among others.

Muller, Eddie, and Faris, Daniel. *Grindhouse: The Forbidden World of "Adults Only" Cinema.* New York, NY: St. Martins Press, 1996. ISBN: 9780312146092.
A history of exploitation movies from the 1930s to 1970s. Filled with photographs, stills, and posters. Includes a section on "Dwain Esper, King of the Roadshows".

Price, Michael H. and Turner, George E. *Forgotten Horrors: The Definitive Edition.* Baltimore, Md: Midnight Marquee Press, 1999. ISBN: 9781887664202.
The authors review various obscure horror movies from the 1930s, like *Revolt of the Zombies* and *The Crime of Doctor Crespi*. Includes a detailed review of *Maniac*.

Price, Michael K. and Turner, George. *Forgotten Horrors 2: Beyond the Horror Ban.* Baltimore, Md: Midnight Marquee Press, 2009. ISBN: 9781887664431.
Includes reviews of the Esper distributed pictures *Forbidden Adventure*, with shades of bestiality, and *Jungle Virgin*.

Puchalski, Steven. *Slimetime: A Guide to Sleazy Mindless Movie Entertainment.* Manchester: Headpress/Critical Vision, 1996. ISBN: 9780952328858.
A very thick guide covering all kinds of exploitation and B-movie, horror, and trash cinema. Includes a review of *Maniac*.

Schaefer, Eric. *"Bold! Daring! Shocking! True!": A History of Exploitation Films, 1919-1959.* London: Duke University Press, 1999. ISBN: 9780822323747.
Covers all kinds of films, from the drug genre to the nudie and vice flicks. Key people like Esper, Kroger Babb, Samuel Cummings, Louis Sonney and J.D. Kendis are all discussed. David F. Friedman gives this book a promotional blurb.

Sheridan, Simon. *Keeping the British End Up: Four Decades of Saucy Cinema.* London: Reynolds and Hearn, 2001. ISBN: 9781903111215.
A detailed history of the British sex and exploitation movies, including modest films like *Naked As Nature Intended* and the *Carry On* series.

Svehela, Gary J. and Svehela, Susan. *Guilty Pleasures of the Horror Film.* Baltimore, Md: Midnight Marquee Press, 1997. ISBN: 9781887664035.
A guide to some of the worst horror films ever made. Bret Wood's very detailed essay on *Maniac* points out that William C. Thompson – the man who shot Ed Wood's first feature film, *Glen or Glenda?* – was also the photographer on *Maniac*.

Wood, Bret. *Marihuana, Motherhood & Madness: Three Screenplays from the Exploitation Cinema of Dwain Esper.* Lanham, Md: Scarecrow Press, 1998. ISBN: 9780810833753.
Bret Wood is the world's foremost expert on the films of Dwain Esper. He includes the screenplays for *Modern Motherhood*, *Maniac*, and *Marihuana*. Each screenplay has extensive notes on the production and the various scenes. Includes the appeal to the censors with specific information about various exploitation films.

The (Un)Hollow Man

Paul Verhoeven Discusses the Politics of Pulp

Xavier Mendik

Fritz Lang made a career out of it. Douglas Sirk changed the nature of authorship theory on the back of it. And Paul Verhoeven has also joined the list of European directors who have gone to Hollywood and subverted the content and clichés of American genre cinema. For Sirk, it was the hyper-sensitised domain of melodrama that was manipulated as a way of commenting on the constraints and tensions within 1950s American society. For Verhoeven, it is the excesses of 'male' genres such as science fiction and the erotic thriller that the director has parodied and played upon in order to send up male sexual identity and the American power-elite. The typical Verhoeven male finds himself in situations in which his sense of identity, sexuality and past, are profoundly undercut by either duplicitous individuals or corrupt social structures. In terms of his representations of sexual difference, Verhoeven's women are repeatedly cast as vamps whose bonds with other females function to further exclude the male from the domains of knowledge and desire. In so doing Verhoeven has established himself as a distinctly 'un-hollow' man, capable of fusing complex intellectual concerns within the remit of popular film.

In this exclusive interview with Cult Film Archive Director Xavier Mendik, Paul Verhoeven discusses the political underpinnings to his Stateside pulp productions as well as revealing the early influences that moulded his life and career.

Xavier Mendik: There seems to be a longstanding tradition of European directors such as Douglas Sirk, who relocate to America and subvert existing Hollywood genre codes. Do you see yourself as part of that tradition?

Paul Verhoeven: I am sure that it is true, but I have not thought about it too much. For instance, there are directors whose work I know better than Douglas Sirk. I am much more aware of Billy Wilder, or Alfred Hitchcock's work than, say, Sirk or Max Ophuls. I was aware of the fact that there were a lot of European directors in the 1960s, 1970s and 1980s that tried to go to the United States and work. However, what you found was that after the failure of one or two American movies they relocated back to Europe. Lina Wertmuller

was there, Truffaut made an American movie, and Antonioni also did one or two American movies. They were all very disappointed in the results and the producers were all very disappointed in the financial results of those films, anyway they relocated away from the United States after that.

Were you worried that a similar fate would befall your Hollywood career?

When I came to the United States, I felt strongly that if I tried to do my own thing I would be on a fast track out of there! I had seen so many other European directors trying to do that and failing. I thought, "If you try and immediately be yourself there, that might not be the best way of getting into the American film industry." So, I was more inclined from the beginning to go with the flow of what was happening. I remember that one of the first times I ever came to the United States, even before I was a resident, a Dutch guy who was working in the video industry recognised me at the airport and said, "Let me give you one piece of advice, go with the flow here. If you try and go against the grain here, you are out!"

above: Exploitation film director Verhoeven has also made serious works inspired by his upbringing during the Second World War, including **Black Book** (*opposite*).

Did the type of genre movies you were being offered ever worry you?

Well, when they offered me **RoboCop**, I was hesitant to do it, because after the kinds of films I had done in Europe, it seemed such a silly movie! The films I was used to making had been much more realistic, dealing with normality, people's problems and situations. Some of these films had been based on autobiographical experiences, and even the ones which people think were not based on personal experience, such as **The Fourth Man**, is in fact 90% autobiographical, strangely enough. So in Europe I was always working more from reality, whereas **RoboCop** was of course completely fantastical.

The temptation surely must have been to alter the film along these European lines.

When I read the script for the film for the first time, I really did not think that the project was for me. But then my wife read it again after me and said I should look at it in a more open-minded way, because it is a film with multiple layers, which I could see would allow me to bring in my own interests. So, when I came to do the film, I immediately started to change the script. I asked to have the relationship between the two central people to be changed to allow Peter Weller's character to have an affair with Nancy Allen. So I guess I wanted to make this film with a European outlook, by making it morally decadent! But then I had this vague intuition that this would make the project *too* much me, so I asked the writers to amend the changes I had made and to go back to the original version they had suggested. I had decided against changing the structure of the screenplay and left the characters relations as they were. I think this was the best intuition of my life; a voice inside my head said, "You are thinking as the European you, and you need to think as the American you, and you should back off!"

*It is interesting that you have identified these layers to genre films like **RoboCop**. This must surely mean that genre movies are very easy to subvert?*

Yes, I think that is true. In the case of **RoboCop**, some of these possibilities were already given in the script, unlike **Starship Troopers**, where I was involved with the writing from the very beginning. So what I did with **RoboCop** was to emphasise, to push certain elements harder than perhaps an American director would have done. I had more pleasure in subverting some of the features of American culture as someone who had just arrived there. So I certainly saw some of the idiotic aspects of this culture, most notably my feelings that television was so different and so banal from the type of European television I had been used to. A lot of the little things that happen in the movie, such as the reporting of crime, was based on my amazement at American television and American life in general. I am not so sure I could do that so well anymore, now after fifteen years of living there, I have lost a certain innocence. I feel that I am now looking at the United States with more of an American eye than a European one.

As your career has progressed, your films appear to have increasingly displayed a very cynical attitude to American society and culture. Would you agree?

Yes, well I feel that it took me a long time to decode what was going on. I think I understood much more about American society after reading Chomsky; that was what basically opened my eyes and I have been reading Chomsky ever since! Before that I didn't get all of the paradigms, which is why I feel that although **RoboCop** *is* subversive, it is not as politically subversive as **Starship Troopers**, which I feel is a far more open attack on American society. **RoboCop** is more of an analysis and criticism of military corporations taking over government through the OCP syndicate. With **Starship Troopers**, that occurred after I had lived there for twelve years and starting to realise what American society and American politics was like. I feel it took me this time to decode the newspapers and the way they report events. I think I had initially taken them far more seriously than they should be taken. I had a hard time to realise that even well respected newspapers like *The New York Times* and *The Washington Post* or even *News Week* and *Time* were not necessarily truthful, but were extremely political in their outlook. By this I mean that they were nearly always trying to make a neo-governmental point; even when they appeared to disagree with an administration they still always went in for government politics. So there did seem to

Oppressive fascist regimes, unstoppable killing machines and rampant military might are recurrent under-pinning themes in Paul Verhoeven's explosive mainstream action movies, which include **Starship Troopers** (*above*) and **RoboCop** (*opposite bottom left*).

me to be a connection between the American media and the government. What I am not saying is that there is a conspiracy theory going on here, rather it is the fact that these people all work in the same direction, whether it's Bush or Clinton in control or whoever.

Does it bother you that many critics have attached an extreme right-wing reading to **Starship Troopers**?

That was mostly based on an article in *The Washington Post*, which was trying neutralise a film that was critical of the United States, by claiming it was fascist. It was that interpretation that was taken over in many of the other European newspapers, without having seen the movie. I noticed that several years later, when I did my tour with **Hollow Man**, the perception of **Starship Troopers** had changed. People are now much more aware of what we had in mind than when the movie came out. I do remember that when the film came out I was attacked in a most belligerent way in ex-fascist countries such as Germany and Italy. Interestingly enough, this didn't happen in England, where the film had a good campaign. Here, there was a big billboard campaign which claimed that, "The only good bug is a dead bug", and these lines from the film were on posters all over London, which I thought was a really

excellent campaign. It partly explains why the film was more successful there than in any other European country. England got the film's message, and I was not criticised at all. I think that people in England got the fact that the film was ironically playing with the structure of American governments, by using fascist imagery in the style of Leni Riefenstahl.

Some critics have argued that the film displayed a very personal agenda for you.

Well, clearly this is based on the fascination with fascism that I have. This is based on the fact that when I was a child, I was living in occupied Holland, where we had to accept German domination and their fascist regime. So as I was growing up, I saw the Germans ordering my parents around. My father was head of a primary school, and was responsible for kids between the ages of six and twelve. The German cavalry had put all of their horses into the quarters of the school and they ordered my father and mother to do things for them and they had no option but to accept their presence there. As a young child that was very difficult to watch and I think that a lot of these memories are essential to what you call my fascination with fascism.

Elizabeth Berkley stars in **Showgirls** (1996), arguably Paul Verhoeven's most controversial film.

Do you feel those memories of occupation left you with a hatred of fascism that now informs your work?

Not just hatred, but a desire to understand what motivates these actions. During the occupation, one of my best friends' parents were heavily pro-Nazi, and at the time, I didn't understand why I was forbidden to play with him. The first girlfriend I had, also had a father with these leanings, so I learned that it was a really bad move to fall in love with that girl! I think these strained relationships certainly fed into my fascination, so I started to read and read about Nazi Germany in order to try and understand. I still don't fully understand what my fascination is, but I know that I share it with a lot of other humans. One of these people is Ian Kershaw, who just spent ten years writing a very big book about Hitler. This begs the question, how can you spend ten years on something so evil? I think the answer is that it is evil and that is what we find so fascinating. Evil, whether it is Satanic or whatever, is far more fascinating than paradise.

Some people argue that fascism is an evil beyond logic and critical interpretation, and should be treated as such.

Yes, but I am very much against those people who want to portray the actions of these fascists as a mystery. There are some people who believe that evil is a concept that can never be explained or fully understood. A very famous Dutch writer named Harry Mulisch recently wrote a book in which he argues that Hitler is frequently compared to a black hole, so his actions are never fully explained or explored. However, I feel that this approach is a mystification and nonsense. You can very clearly study the history of the Third Reich and understand why it happened, how it happened, what Hitler wanted and so on. By critically thinking it through, not only can it be understood, but also it can more fully be compared with other events. For instance, I see a gradual erosion of the distance between the Holocaust and the destiny of the Armenians, as well

as a growing connection between the Holocaust and the killing in Rwanda, for example. I refuse to see one as essentially different from the other. A recent book was published entitled *The Holocaust Industry,* and this considers the way in which the Holocaust has been bracketed off as a special kind of evil. This is something which I feel should not be done. You cannot talk about two kinds of suffering. You cannot say that, "This is a unique kind of suffering and the other ones are secondary kinds of suffering." I strongly disagree with this. There should not be a monopoly on suffering.

Moving from the social to the sexual, your films have often been misinterpreted as pandering to masculine desires. How do you feel about such readings?

I have never understood these interpretations. I mean, I could understand why people might think or see **Starship Troopers** as fascist, because it is clearly quoting from **Triumph of the Will**. So if the film is taken literally, I guess it would be possible to say that it somehow admires Adolf Hitler. But I have never understood why anyone would call me anti-feminine. Actually, I think that I portray the women in my films as very strong characters, even when they are evil. I am a very big fan of women, even down to feeling more comfortable in the company of women than men, so to be branded as chauvinistic is something I don't understand at all.

this page: Verhoeven explores his understandable fascination with Nazi occupation in **Black Book** (2006).

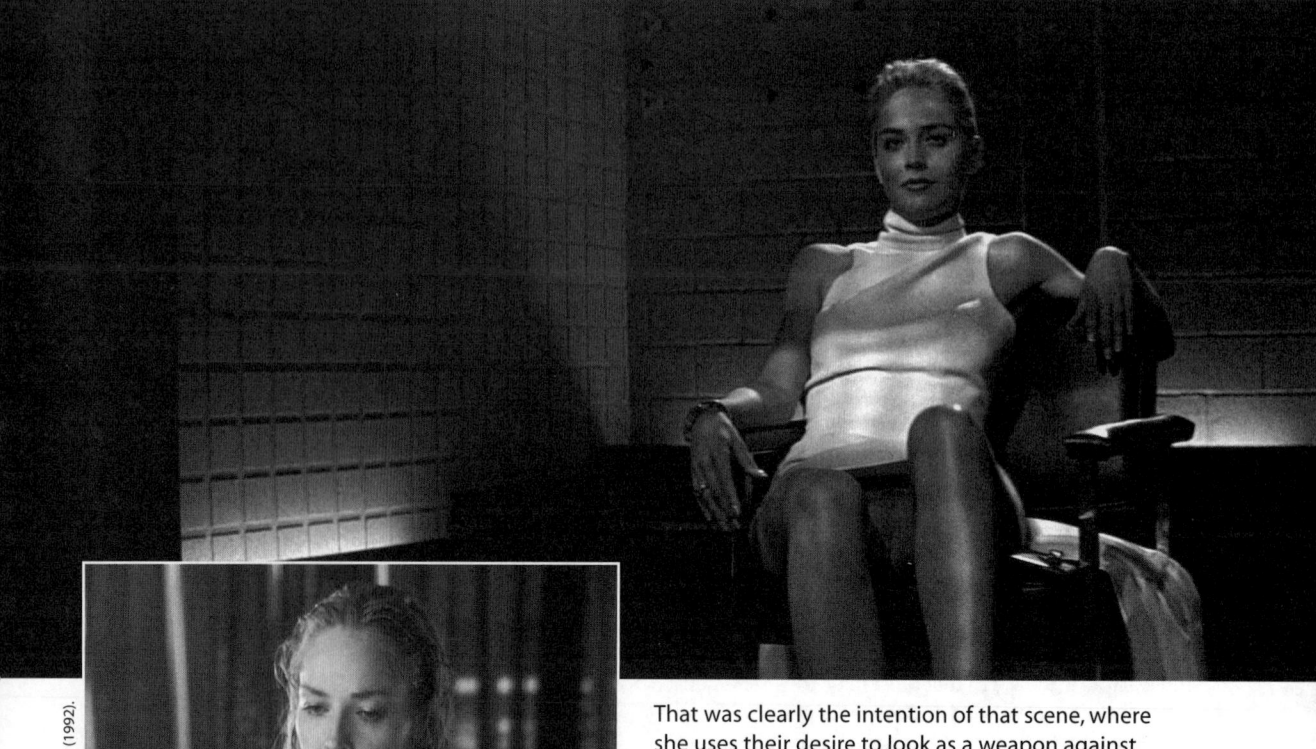

Sharon Stone's iconic performance in Paul Verhoeven's **Basic Instinct** (1992).

What is odd about your women, is that they create these female groups that exclude and even feminise the male characters that surround them. Even a film like **Basic Instinct**, with its famous beaver shot seems to be manipulating, exposing and disempowering male sexual obsession.

That was clearly the intention of that scene, where she uses their desire to look as a weapon against them. So by showing them glimpses of her vagina, she effectively reduces these men to zero. Following the release of the film, there was a big controversy with Sharon Stone where she disavowed that shot, claiming she did not know about the angle, whatever. However, I would say that this is not being truthful, as it would not be possible to shoot such a scene without the actors knowing. Also, she saw the shot afterwards. Before she and her managers felt that the shot would harm her career, Sharon was absolutely fascinated about the scene. We discussed it at dinner with her before we shot it, where I presented it to her as a possibility of something that happened to me when I was a student. There was a woman in our circuit that was always doing this. And my friends went up to her at a party and said, "Do you know that we can see right inside your legs, and see everything there." And she replied, "Of course, that's why I do that!" I told that story to Sharon at dinner, as it was already clarified in the script that she was already naked at the beach house, when it is clear that she has nothing under her dress. Later in the car, she says to Michael Douglas, "You know that I don't wear underwear." These two scenes were at the beginning and the end of the interrogation scene. So I said to her, "Why don't we look in the middle of the conversation when you sit directly in front of these four or five people, why do we not just show that you are not wearing anything". And she said, "That is great". We both really liked that idea, and I still think it was highly inspired. She realised that those actions would give her so much power in that scene, and that these people would be drooling at her feet. She realised that by showing them her body, she would be in command from here in and that she could turn the interrogation against them. Sharon is a very, very clever girl and she turned in a brilliant performance. It was only later that she got afraid, that her performance would be hurt by the way in which Americans judge morality. She clearly felt that what could be a big success for her would be diminished by that scene, and that's why she freaked out. And that was mainly because the people around her freaked out, but I refused to change that, even after she insisted that I change it and even threatened to sue me if I didn't. It took her about seven or eight years to acknowledge that I was right not to alter the scene, as she now seems to suggest in interviews.

Beyond your depiction of women, your work seems to be very much concerned with the homoerotic tensions in masculinity.

Well, it was always there in my Dutch movies, such as **The Fourth Man**. So from my earliest work you can see that I have always discussed homosexuality. Even if you look at **Basic Instinct**, you will see that I portray homosexuality as a central part of society. What I did in that film was not to treat it as an issue, which would have been wrong, but rather I used it as a plot mechanism. I felt this was the best thing to do in order to make a pro-gay statement. I think that in my films if the characters were heterosexual or homosexual the plot would still work because their sexual orientation informs the plot. So many movies about homosexuality choose to make it an issue rather than a plot point and many of them produce anti-gay comments as a result. Growing up in Holland, with its tolerance of the gay community, and then later working with so many cast and crew that were homosexual gave me a good perspective on this issue. Anyway, I actually think that we are all born bisexual and it is only really in adolescence that our sexual futures are decided. It is really only Christianity that has fucked us all over with its condemnations of homosexuality, and that still haunts us even today. If you look at the very sophisticated and civilised layers of ancient Greek society, there was no problem with homosexuality at all. So I do think that it is Christianity that has fucked us all over!

Xavier Mendik wishes to offer his sincere thanks to Paul Verhoeven for all his interest and enthusiasm, as well as the staff at the Brussels International Festival of Fantasy Film for arranging the interview.

Xavier Mendik is Director of the *Cine-Excess* International Film Festival and DVD label at Brunel University, and has written extensively on cult and horror traditions. Some of his publications in this area include *The Cult Film Reader* (2008), *Alternative Europe: Eurotrash and Exploitation Cinema Since 1945* (2004), *Shocking Cinema of the Seventies* (2002), *Underground USA: Filmmaking Beyond the Hollywood Canon* (2002) and *Dario Argento's Tenebrae* (2000). Xavier Mendik has just edited a volume on erotic cinema entitled *Peep Shows: Cult Film and the Cine-Erotic* for Columbia University Press and is completing a monograph on 1970s Italian cult film for 2011. Beyond his academic writing, Xavier Mendik has an established profile as a documentary filmmaker and distributor. He was responsible for the recent high-definition UK restoration of Dario Argento's **Suspiria** for the Nouveaux Pictures-Cine-Excess DVD label, and has recently directed the documentary 'The Long Road Back From Hell', intended for inclusion on the Shameless Films 2011 UK Director's Cut of **Cannibal Holocaust**.

Further details of Xavier's activities can be found here: www.cine-excess.co.uk

top: Original Dutch poster for Verhoeven's striking international breakthrough feature, **The Fourth Man** (1983).

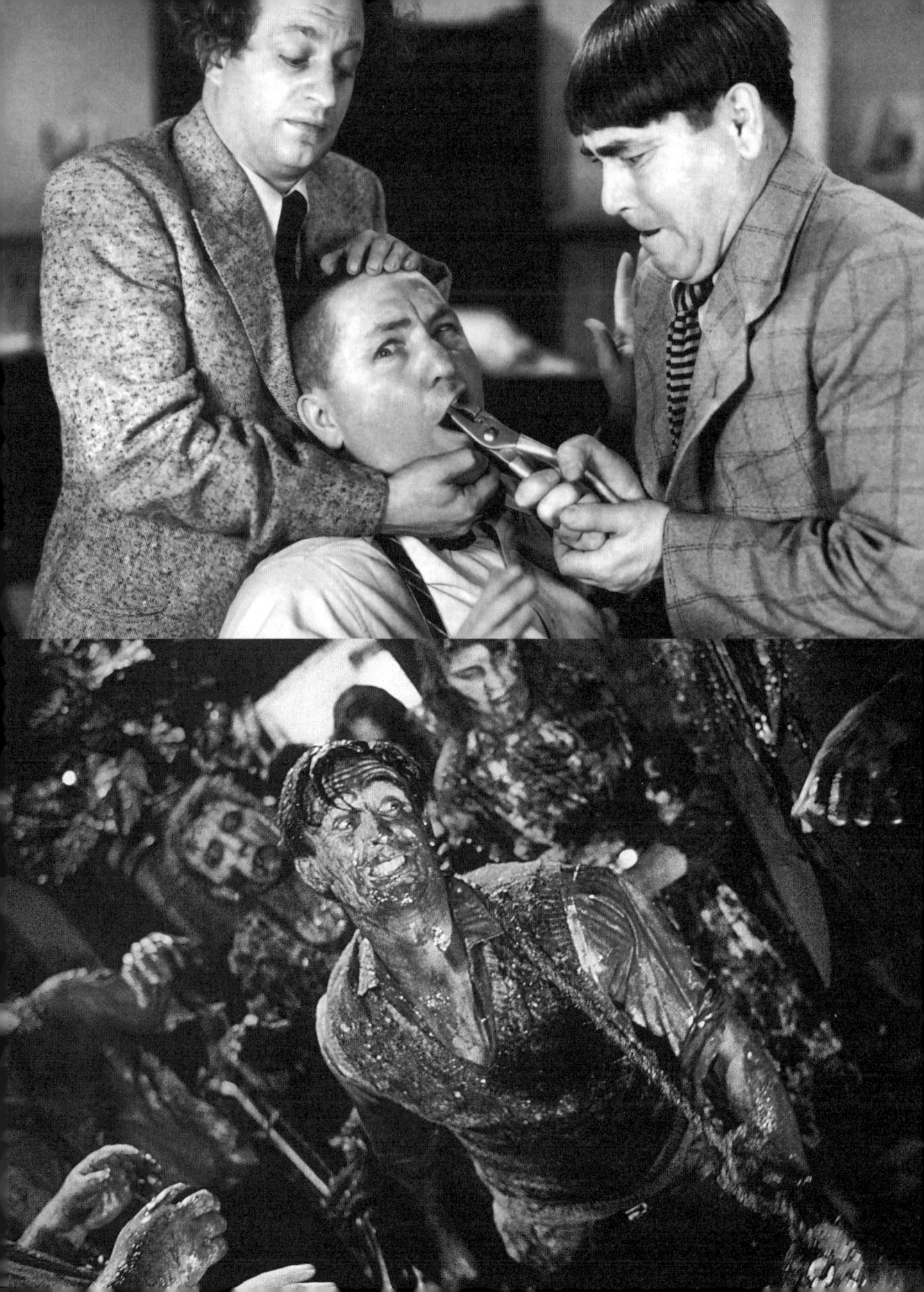

The Gore the Merrier

Slapstick, "Splatstick" and Body Horror

Jamie Russell

"I never saw anything funny that wasn't terrible.
If it causes pain it's funny; if it doesn't, it isn't"
– W.C. Fields

In the Encyclopedia of Human Misery, poor old Ash (Bruce Campbell) has an entry all to himself. After decapitating his possessed girlfriend Linda in **Evil Dead 2: Dead By Dawn** (1987), the lantern-jawed Everydude no doubt deserved a break. But in the **Evil Dead** series, there's no such thing as time out. Minutes after leaving Linda to rest in pieces, his right hand starts beating him up and breaking assorted pieces of kitchen crockery over his head. Understandably exasperated by the sheer unfairness of it all, Ash reaches for his trusty chainsaw and prepares to perform an auto-amputation while screaming "Who's laughing now?!"

Well we are, that's for sure. Sam Raimi's splatterfest sequel-cum-remake plays like the bastard offspring of a Video Nasty crossed with a Laurel and Hardy two-reeler. Scampering away to the jaunty tones of Joe LoDuca's '20s style soundtrack, Ash's hand darts in and out of mouse holes, flips its fuming owner "The Bird" and giggles to itself like a Jawa on crystal meth. After taking a few pot-shots with his shotgun, Ash finally traps it under a bucket weighted down with (ahem) a copy of Ernest Hemingway's **A Farewell to Arms**.

Inspired by turns by Thing from **The Addams Family;** co-writer Scott Spiegel's juvenile Super-8 short **Attack of the Helping Hand** (a spoof on a popular US TV advert for Hamburger Helper); and deadly digits classic **The Beast with Five Fingers** (1946), this demented comedy-horror sequence also owes a debt to classic slapstick comedy. It's the high-water mark of a much-ignored trend in horror cinema that sporadically flourished between the late-1970s and early-1990s and has been belatedly dubbed "splatstick".

The history of splatstick begins with George A. Romero's zombie masterpiece **Dawn of the Dead** (1978).

Comedy/horror cross-over films such as **Evil Dead 2: Dead By Dawn** (*above*), **Dawn of the Dead** (*below*) and **Braindead** (*opposite bottom*) all owe a debt to The Three Stooges (*opposite top*).

In the final third of this seemingly bleak apocalyptic tale, Romero stages an audacious climactic battle between zombies, bikers and the film's three surviving protagonists. As the bikers storm the empty mall and open up the gates to the lumbering zombies, Romero jettisons his earlier satirical seriousness in favour of all-out comedy, with bikers throwing custard pies at their antagonists. It's a reworking of the classic slapstick food fight for the grindhouse.

กล้าท้าได้ว่า คุณไม่เคยพบผีดุเท่านี้ ในชีวิต

EVIL DEAD

After **Dawn of the Dead**, splatstick began to surface in a wide variety of low-budget horror movies including: the **Evil Dead** trilogy (**The Evil Dead** (1982), **Evil Dead 2: Dead By Dawn** (1987), **Army of Darkness** (1993)), the **Re-Animator** series (**Re-Animator** (1985), **Bride of Re-Animator** (1990), **Beyond Re-Animator** (2003)), Peter Jackson's **Bad Taste** (1987) and **Braindead** (1992) and, in an early incarnation, Frank Henenlotter's **Basket Case** (1982). Despite this impressive list though, splatstick's distinctive blend of comedy, entrails and chainsaws has rarely been given much attention by critics. Most have dismissed the trend as nothing more than a puerile reworking of the splatter movie.

By and large, no one has paid much attention to splatstick's other roots: the *slapstick* comedy of early Hollywood. Like its comedy cousin, splatstick horror treats the physical realm of bodies and objects with great scepticism. Both seek to prove that the physical world of flesh and objects is never as certain – nor as forgiving – as we might like to pretend.

above: Even the intestines of a decapitated corpse can take on a murderous life of their own in a splatstick movie such as **Re-Animator** (1985).

Slapstick, the Body and the Perversity of Objects

Pain and misery was always the chief focus of slapstick comedy. The genre takes its name from the buffoonery of the Italian *commedia dell'arte* of the 16th Century, where Harlequin carried a variation of the jester's baton known as a "slap stick". Shaped like a wooden sword, with a split running lengthways down the middle, the stick was Harlequin's weapon of choice because of the satisfying "slap" it produced when he hit his hapless victims. It was painful stuff and as slapstick evolved into cuffs and pratfalls it was rarely a picnic for the performers involved. They were frequently left physically scarred by the pursuit of belly-laughs. In his book *Slapstick! The Illustrated Story of Knockabout Comedy*, historian Tony Staveacre writes:

> "The line between the 'nap' which is pulled (which doesn't hurt) and 'straight nap' (which does) is a very fine one, and the road to the audience's heart is littered with broken limbs and damaged organs […] In the nineteenth century, Gustave Fréjaville described a French clown whose left cheek – having been too often 'caressed', had become as dry as parchment, and whose left eye revealed a detached retina caused by the repeated shock of professional cuffing."[1]

Hollywood slapstick clowning grew out of this kind of comedy and its threat of physical injury. Obsessed with confronting the body's vulnerability, inefficiency and messy reality, slapstick performers like Chaplin, Keaton and Lloyd got laughs by reminding their audience that fleshy existence was a source of abject embarrassment. As comedy historian Alan Dale notes, "The essence of a slapstick gag is a physical assault on, or collapse of, the hero's dignity".[2]

One only has to recall Oliver Hardy's repeated bashings (hitting his fingers while trying to hammer nails, falling off ladders, being struck on the head by planks and bricks) to see how slapstick deflates the egos of its protagonists by showing its heroes – and the audience – that their bodies can't be relied on. Compare that with Bruce Campbell's impotent rage as he realises that his *own hand* is giving him the finger... Suffering indignities is the stock in trade of slapstick heroes.

At heart, slapstick was all about the downside of living in a physical world. As Dale explains:

> "[Slapstick is] a fundamental, universal and eternal response to the fact that life is physical. Of the two components, body and soul, we have empirical proof of the first alone. It's

the body that we can *see* interacting with physical forces and objects, and our intense exasperation that this interaction doesn't run smoother […] stimulates the urge to tell a story in a slapstick mode."*3*

A central part of such frustration was built around what Dale calls "the triumph of the *thing*".*4* Objects in the slapstick universe never act (or react) the way they ought to. Instead, they develop a life of their own. Ladders, buckets, hosepipes and doorknobs can't be trusted. They gang up on the hero, tripping him up, falling on his head and generally getting in his way. Slapstick was never interested in the safety of objects, only their cruelty. The slapstick protagonist was always the whipping boy of the inanimate world. "The rule was that inanimate objects held important positions and developed preferences of their own," wrote film critic Siegfried Kracauer in an essay on silent film comedy in *Sight & Sound* in 1951. "More often than not they were filled with a certain malice towards anything human".*5*

While slapstick never claimed to offer any great social commentary, it's obvious that this fear of objects and disappointment with the body was a veritable product of its time. It captured the changing relationship between people and machines that the industrialized landscape of early 20th Century America was experiencing. Slapstick comedy was, in some

respects, a response to man's altered sense of his role in the world. In the modernized, mechanized work place – like the factory setting of Chaplin's **Modern Times** (1936) – man was no longer master of his environment. Instead he was an expendable, fleshy cog in a machine geared towards productivity, efficiency and automation.

In the early part of the 20th Century, the fashionable text for workplace managers was Frederick Taylor's *The Principles of Scientific Management* (1911). It had a keen sense of the body's shortcomings. Well aware of the disparity between the smooth-running operation of industrial machinery and the messy inefficiency of the human bodies needed to maintain and supervise it, the time-motion studies underpinning Taylorism even prescribed the frequency and duration of toilet visits (something Chaplin satirized in **Modern Times** in the scene where his hero sneaks off to the lavatories for a quick cigarette, only to be chased out by the factory supervisor who's captured him skiving on a surveillance camera).

The physical comedy of slapstick was both an anarchic rejection of these attempts to regulate the body and a tacit admission that the clumsy human vessel was as inefficient and undignified as the Taylorists claimed. Blending comedy with a touch of horror, slapstick let its audience laugh at the awful, awkward realities of their own flesh.

above: Charlie Chaplin finds that he has become a literal fleshy cog in the machine in **Modern Times** (1936).

From Slap to Splat: The Evolution of a Genre

No matter what indignities the slapstick hero was made to suffer, it was always a safe bet that he would survive to slip on another banana peel. In *splatstick* horror, such certainties no longer apply. While the worst injuries that Oliver Hardy ever endured on-screen were black eyes or bumps on the head, the splatstick hero faces dismemberment, possession, death and the unflinching realization that his body is an alien entity that isn't necessarily under his control.

That's not to say that splatstick isn't funny. For filmmakers like Raimi, Jackson and Stuart **Re-Animator** Gordon, the key to the gore lies in playing up the inherent horror of slapstick comedy. In interviews, Raimi has pointed out the links between his work on **The Evil Dead** series and the slapstick tradition:

> "The Three Stooges were a great influence on [**The Evil Dead**] … When the light bulb fills up with blood and the blood comes out of the sockets, there's a Stooges episode called 'A Plumbing We Will Go' [where] they hook up all the pipes and it fills the light bulbs with water and they hook up the water supply to the electrical system. The gas ring pours water and out of the television pours water, so I just took that idea and entirely changed it to horror – they're so close anyway. The Stooges are *so* violent."*6*

In **The Evil Dead**, there's a deliriously skewered comedic logic to events, as if the writer-director had crossbred The Three Stooges with **The Exorcist** in some dark basement laboratory. The resulting hybrid

is full of broad, knockabout comedy *and* scenes of gory horror undercut by Joe LoDuca's inappropriately upbeat soundtrack. For every dismemberment by chainsaw, there's a pratfall. For every exploding wound, there's a sight gag. As the blood splashes across the screen, Raimi uses the language of both slapstick and horror in innovative ways – fountains of pus act like old-fashioned soda siphons, while buckets of blood take the place of whitewash. Where slapstick heroes had to deal with objects that merely seemed recalcitrant, Ash has to battle objects that are literally possessed by malicious spirits – in one scene in **Evil Dead 2** every household object in the cabin comes to life (books, chairs, moose heads, lamps) to laugh at him.

From Raimi's perspective, the demented comedy of **Evil Dead 2** was a direct response to the vitriol he faced over the original **Evil Dead**. After his low-budget horror movie was banned as a Video Nasty in the UK and dragged through the courts, Raimi was left reeling. Amazed that anyone could take **The Evil Dead**'s overblown scenes of decapitation, popped eyeballs and dismemberment even remotely seriously, the director turned his attention to **Evil Dead 2**. With almost exactly the same plot and characters, **Evil Dead 2** was not so much a sequel as an exaggerated remake in which Raimi ratcheted up every facet of the original film, partly in an attempt to prove to the moral majority that **The Evil Dead** was always meant to be read as a comedy.

above: Head in a vice... Sam Raimi has always stated that the **Evil Dead** films were primarily influenced by The Three Stooges, as amply demonstrated here.

Raimi's experience was well-noted by his peers. Many realized that this kind of splatstick horror – when played to excess as in **Evil Dead 2** – could lessen the wrath of the censors'. Peter Jackson claims his outrageous splatstick film **Braindead** (aka **Dead Alive**) won over the BBFC by using similar tactics:

"Someone told me that the English censor said he wasn't going to cut **Braindead** because he refused to take the film seriously. While **Braindead** is a very gory movie, and may or may not be the bloodiest film ever made as some people say, it just goes to show that making a film funny will always make it much easier for the censor. I mean a film like **Henry: Portrait of a Serial Killer**, which contained very little humour, certainly didn't help itself at all." **7**

Seeing as **Braindead** features, among other gory moments, a man chasing a zombie toddler before beating it senseless against a metal railing, one might have expected the BBFC to reach for the "REJECT" stamp. Yet, as Jackson points out, that sequence styled itself on a recognizable comic tradition: "It's a very Buster Keaton, slapstick kind of scene". Judging by the later careers of both Raimi and Jackson – directing big budget blockbuster adaptations of **Spider-Man** and the **Lord of the Rings** trilogy respectively – one could argue that making splatstick movies is less of a hindrance to mainstream success than making "straight" horror movies like **Henry: Portrait of a Serial Killer** might be.

Splatstick is more than a simple homage to slapstick, though. It's also comedy with an edge. Expanding upon the fleshy anxieties of its cultural cousin, splatstick horror takes the physical "slaps" of slapstick and turns them into "splats" – bloody SFX sequences in which we see the body in all its gory glory. Latex gore lets splatstick go beyond the bounds of silent comedy to discover a hilarious, yet horrific, universe in which bodies become objects and take on a terrifying life of their own. Even Buster Keaton's stony-faced stoicism might have cracked if someone had ripped his stomach out mid-pratfall.

WINGNUT FILMS presents

BAD TASTE

Starring PETE O'HERNE, MIKE MINETT, TERRY POTTER, CRAIG SMITH, PETER JACKSON, DOUG WRENN, DEAN LAWRIE, KEN HAMMON
Written by PETER JACKSON Additional Script TONY HILES and KEN HAMMON
Music MICHELLE SCULLION Post-Production Supervisor JAMIE SELKIRK Sound Mix BRENT BURGE
Consultant Producer TONY HILES Produced and Directed by PETER JACKSON

Bodies are always being pulled apart in splatstick horror. Slapstick comedy's belief that the body is messily inefficient and frustratingly unruly isn't enough for these horror filmmakers. They want to prove the point as graphically as possible. So, Ash ends up chasing his recalcitrant hand in **Evil Dead 2**; **Bad Taste**'s Derek (director Peter Jackson himself) has to face the ignominy of stuffing bits of his brain tissue back into his skull after a crack on the head; and **Re-Animator**'s Dr. Hill (David Gale) is brought back to life as a decapitated corpse.

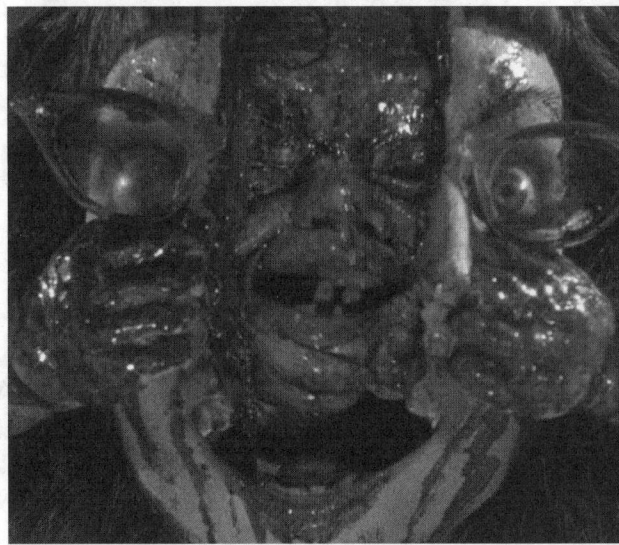

above: Bodies in revolt, or just revolting bodies? Stuart Gordon's **Re-Animator** (*left*) and Peter Jackson's **Braindead** (*right*) delight in overt displays of fleshy chaos.

the body, splatstick obsessively reveals the messy reality that lies beneath. We're forced to confront our bodies as monstrous, alien vessels that we are trapped inside.

Of course, there's always more than a dash of humour underlying the horror of such sequences. Partly this is because of the sheer audacity of the special effects teams in conceiving and executing such grisly scenes of physical injury. Yet, the comedy is also a result of these films' keen sense of the comical ignominy of physical existence. Just as Oliver Hardy was resigned to the fact that life was a never-ending series of blows and pratfalls, so the splatstick protagonist recognizes that the body is an awkward and messy chunk of flesh. In the **Re-Animator** films, Dr. Hill's decapitated corpse is left in an unenviable position as his petulant, impatient severed head shouts instructions to his blind, clumsy body as it knocks into walls, trips over furniture and acts in a generally exasperating manner. As a nightmare image of the Cartesian dichotomy of mind and body made literal, Dr. Hill proves what any student of slapstick comedy knows only too well: that the physical body is nothing short of an indignity foisted upon us by the capricious forces of evolution (or, if you're not in the Dawkins camp, a clearly psychotic and sadistic God).

Splatstick characters are frequently forced into the position of spectators, watching as their bodies, or body parts, become objects with an autonomous life of their own. Making the body into an object and imbuing it with perverse life is a recurrent theme of splatstick horror – epitomized by the eviscerated entrails of **Braindead**, which slither around with a murderous will of their own while the attached anus farts from such out-of-body exertions. Delving into

Is it telling that splatstick peaked in the '80s and '90s? I think so. Just as slapstick can be seen as a reaction to the increasing mechanization of the world in general and the workplace in particular during the first part of the 20th Century, so splatstick can be read as part of a response to a very different set of social and historical circumstances: the AIDS crisis. With their images of bodies turning against their owners, becoming "possessed" and acting in completely alien ways, these films offer horrific images of the flesh running out of control.

HERBERT WEST HAS A VERY GOOD HEAD ON HIS SHOULDERS –

AND ANOTHER ONE IN A DISH ON HIS DESK

H. P. LOVECRAFT'S CLASSIC TALE OF HORROR

RE-ANIMATOR

DEATH IS JUST THE BEGINNING...

Combining a sense of the body's own innate strangeness (something closely related to the HIV virus's ability to turn the body's immune system against the subject) and graphic images of the body's messy reality (blood, pus, vomit – all the bodily fluids that the discourse of AIDS has made even more abject than they previously were), the splatstick genre was undoubtedly shaped by the crisis. The response itself, though, is rather uncertain. Do these riotous gore-fests reinforce an ancient, conservative, puritan hatred of the flesh? Or does the extreme imagery of bodies being opened up, cut to pieces and turned inside out offer a kind of carnivalesque excess, a representation of the body that can't be contained within "normal" mainstream images of the corporeal?

Travelling to the Brink

Breaking through boundaries was a key part of slapstick comedy's power. In the 1950s, Kracauer likened the formal arrangement of slapstick to a scattergun blast of gags and pratfalls. This was, he argued, potentially liberating, since such anarchy had little use for the conventions of linear storytelling, basing itself instead on a series of outrageous segments rather than a complete "whole". As a result, slapstick was one of the most "modern" styles of cinema, capturing the shocking, disjointed nature of contemporary existence.

> "Any such gag was a small unit complete in itself and any comedy was a package of gags which, in music hall fashion, were autonomous entities rather than parts of a story. As a rule, there was a story of a sort, but it had merely the function of stringing these monad-like units together. What counted was that they succeeded each other uninterruptedly, not that their succession implemented some plot. To be sure, they often happened to build up a halfway consistent intrigue, yet the intrigue was never of so exacting nature that its significance would have encroached on that of the units composing it […] Film comedy was an ack-ack of gags."*8*

For Kracauer, the machine gun ack-ack of gags assaulted the audience as well as narrative storytelling. You were left dizzy by the frenetic pace. You contorted with laughter. You were shaken and shocked:

> "Film comedy evoked material life at its crudest. And since in those anarchic days of the immobile camera life on the screen was synonymous with life in motion, the comedy makers did their utmost to exaggerate all natural movements. With the aid of a single camera trick they set humanity racing and revelled in games of speed […] It was cinema; it was fun; it was as if you sat in a roller coaster driving ahead at full blast, with your stomach all upside down. The dizziness happily added to the shock effects from disasters and seeming collisions."*9*

Kracauer is actually talking here about the high-speed chases of the Keystone Cops, but it's a description that (decades later) seems readily applicable to Sam Raimi's updated ultra-kinetic camerawork in the **Evil Dead** films. Kracauer read

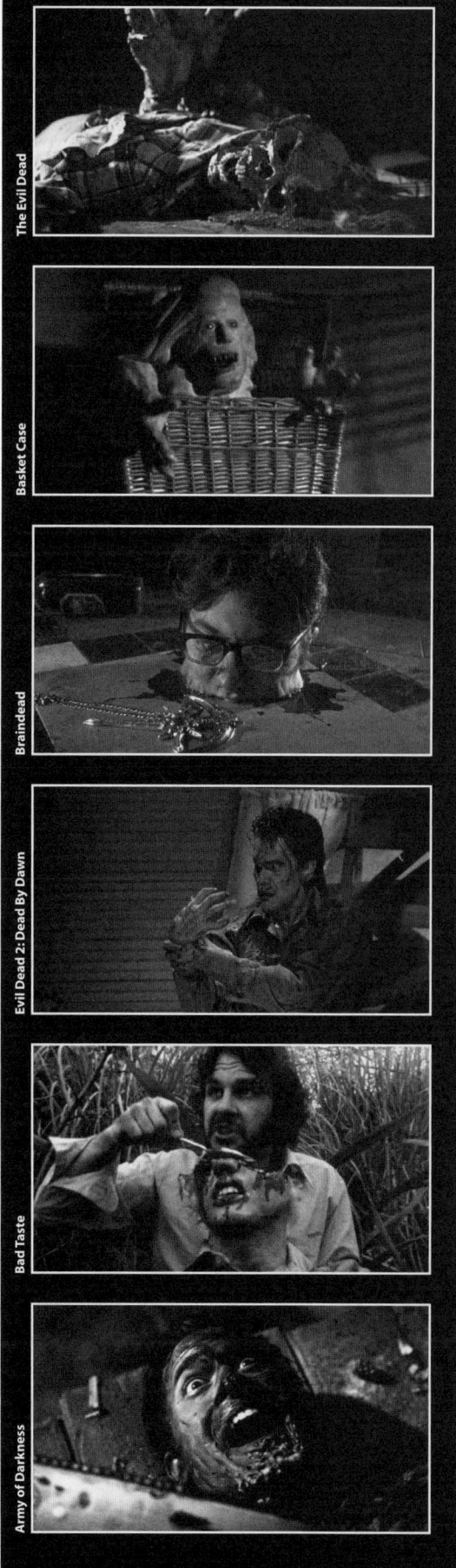

The Evil Dead

Basket Case

Braindead

Evil Dead 2: Dead By Dawn

Bad Taste

Army of Darkness

slapstick as a modernist example of shock and disjunction. What would he have made of Raimi's films with their homemade Steadicam (a camera mounted on a piece of two by four) taking the audience on a white-knuckle ride through demonic woods like a whirling dervish?

At the same time, splatstick also draws on the anarchic formal arrangements of silent film comedy, piling on the decapitations, eviscerations and amputations with little regard for conventional narrative structure. Spectacle is more important than story; the coherence of the movie is hacked up just as surely as the bodies of the players.

Kracauer claimed that slapstick was "an endless action" dominated by "the play with danger, with catastrophe and its prevention in the nick of time" as comedians like Chaplin and Keaton took audiences to "the brink of the abyss".[10] In comparison, splatstick isn't happy with teetering on the brink. It takes us down into the abyss where bodies don't just revolt against us, they also revolt us. It confronts us with the awful truth

of our hapless, hopeless flesh and asks us to chortle at an absurd universe that can create such stunted, crippled creatures. It's a wack-wack-wah that sticks in the throat: who's laughing now?

Jamie Russell is a busy freelance film critic, and the author of the best-selling FAB Press publication *Book of the Dead: The Complete History of Zombie Cinema*.

footnotes

1   Tony Staveacre, *Slapstick! The Illustrated Story of Knockabout Comedy* (London: Angus and Robertson, 1987), p.43.
2   Alan Dale, *Comedy Is a Man in Trouble: Slapstick in American Movies* (Minneapolis and London: University of Minnesota Press, 2000), p.3.
3   *Ibid.*, p.11.
4   *Ibid.*, p.30. My emphasis.
5   Siegfried Kracauer, "Silent Film Comedy" *Sight & Sound* 21/1 (Aug-Sep, 1951), p.31.
6   Sam Raimi quoted in Phil Edwards and Alan Jones, "The Evil Dead Speak: An Interview with Sam Raimi and Robert Tapert", *Starburst* 57 (May, 1983), 29.
7   Peter Jackson quoted in Michael Helms, "Action Jackson", *Fangoria* 121 (April, 1993), p.29.
8   Kracauer, p.32.
9   *Ibid.*, p.31.
10   Siegfried Kracauer, *Marseilles Notebooks*. Cited by Miriam Bratu Hansen in her introduction to Kracauer, *Theory of Film: The Redemption of Physical Reality* (1960. Princeton: Princeton University Press, 1997), p.xxii.

Blood and Roses

Roger Vadim's Erotic Vampire Classic Reassessed

Rocket Mortenson

Long considered a candy-coated approximation of the vampire myth and one of Roger Vadim's weaker films, there's a growing case for **Blood and Roses** in the pantheon of fantastic cinema. Viewed in retrospect, it can be seen as an elegant and highly stylized fantasy, one of only a handful of movies to successfully translate the eroticism of Sheridan Le Fanu's *Carmilla* to screen.

It was a different story in 1961. Then, in the wake of Hammer's swashbuckling approach to their adaptation of *Dracula*, **Blood and Roses** (aka **Et mourir de plaisir**) was viewed as softcore titillation and bit of a snooze. Brazen, perhaps, but hardly a proper horror programmer. Director Vadim, trapped somewhere between commercial dictates and art-house pretension, between the old guard's conservatism and the French New Wave, was accused of sacrificing gory detail for sensual interlude.

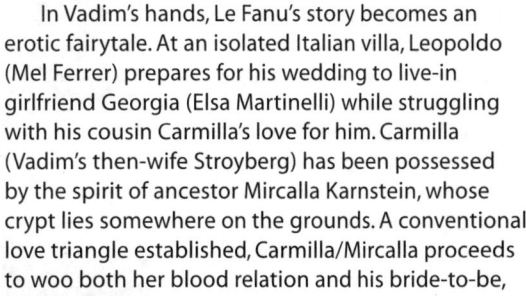

Not that this criticism is entirely baseless. From the opening credits, Vadim's art-school intentions are apparent, Le Fanu's title jettisoned in favour of the ambiguous **Blood and Roses**. Annette Stroyberg (Carmilla) and fellow actress Elsa Martinelli are presented as delicate flowers

in a garden of love and death. It's no accident that the picture's most controversial scene, a thunderstorm embrace between the two women in a greenhouse, embodies this concept so completely. It's one of the defining moments of homoerotic cinema – the glass walls of the hothouse running with condensation as the rain-soaked girls exchange a kiss in the foreground.

It's disturbing to recall how controversial (and brutally censored) this sequence was, bloodshed more acceptable than gay interaction. No mere dramatic invention, the sequence reflects the picture's thematic heart, Carmilla's touch wilting those flowers with which she comes into contact, unrequited love being her greatest curse. One could certainly argue that roses, a widely accepted symbol of heterosexual romanticism, have no choice but to reject her, destroying themselves in the face of lesbian desire.

In Vadim's hands, Le Fanu's story becomes an erotic fairytale. At an isolated Italian villa, Leopoldo (Mel Ferrer) prepares for his wedding to live-in girlfriend Georgia (Elsa Martinelli) while struggling with his cousin Carmilla's love for him. Carmilla (Vadim's then-wife Stroyberg) has been possessed by the spirit of ancestor Mircalla Karnstein, whose crypt lies somewhere on the grounds. A conventional love triangle established, Carmilla/Mircalla proceeds to woo both her blood relation and his bride-to-be, alternately pouty and predatory. She is eventually staked, not by some act of the principals, but during a climactic demolition exercise that propels her through a wooden fence post. At this point, Mircalla reincarnates, this time in the lovely Georgia.

Vadim and co-screenwriter Roger Vailland are more concerned with possession, body and soul, than the act of vampirism. There is no neck biting (or even nibbling) to speak of. In fact, the paraphernalia of the vampire mythos has been largely discarded, along with healthy portions of Le Fanu's 1871 story. While such disparate elements as its fireworks display and masked ball are retained, it's the possession/love story that informs both.

Like Stoker's later *Dracula* (1897), the literary Carmilla personified sexual instability. Assaulting the family order, particularly in relation to Victorian ideals, she procreated through sexual perversion, establishing a stable of slaughtered innocents.

The 'Blood' of the film's title thus sinisterly references Ferrer's obsession with Stroyberg, and their incestuous desire for each other. As Ferrer intones: "The Karnsteins are not a family who have ever managed to be happy on their own. I don't know what would have happened to me if I hadn't met Georgia. She saved me… from myself."

In many ways, Mircalla is the fear of female sexuality incarnate. Her archetypal succubus embodies not only homosexual and incestuous desire, but necrophilic.

It's of more than passing interest, for example, that Mircalla not only desires Georgia, but ultimately possesses her body (and, through this act, Leopoldo).

It's to Vadim's credit that **Blood and Roses** maintains its elegance in the face of such racy symbolism. The only nudity, briefly glimpsed, occurs during a black and white dream sequence that is the picture's highlight. An obvious homage to Jean Cocteau, particularly his **Orpheus** (1950), it telegraphs the film's inspiration.

Having no French horror tradition to draw from, Vadim substitutes Cocteau's artful fantasy. As Carmilla bends over the sleeping Georgia, colour drains from the frame. The ensuing dream/hallucination uses strategically placed splashes of red to punctuate the black and white images, nearly thirty years before this became a fixture of rock video. Carmilla's dress runs with the blood of her victims; Georgia witnesses a medical procedure involving a red-gloved staff (referencing Georges Franju's 1960 **Les yeux sans visage** (aka **Eyes Without a Face**)). At one point, poeticism run amuck, a victim floats by French doors and draws Georgia into the watery netherworld beyond.

It's interesting to compare Vadim's approach to that of his English contemporary, Terence Fisher, who had made such a splash with **Dracula** (aka **Horror of Dracula**, 1958). Having a heritage of horror, both written and cinematic, from which to draw, Fisher had fashioned a string of successful Gothics by 1961 and was regarded (and reviled) as the quintessential genre director. His groundbreaking approach single-handedly revived not only the British film industry, but also the horror film.

It's all the more intriguing, then, that Fisher's **The Brides of Dracula** (1960), his first vampire foray since **Dracula**, would mirror **Blood and Roses** in so many ways.

Both films, for example, begin with narration, a fact that speaks to their fairytale conceits, the stories then unfolding with Brothers Grimm precision. **Brides** tells the tale of Baron Meinster, a foppish young man chained in an isolated castle by his own family. When he's unwittingly released by a visiting teacher (the French Yvonne Monlaur), his first act is to drain his mother.

The script by committee here touches on some of the same themes as **Blood and Roses**. In a sequence both touching and tragic, the Baroness Meinster acknowledges culpability for her necrophilic/incestuous son's behaviour before being dispatched by Van Helsing, the lone holdover from Stoker's novel.

Here is where the divergence begins. In Fisher's world, good and evil are always clearly defined. Behaviours that assault the Victorian morality code, particularly with regard to sexual roles, are punished. Baroness Meinster welcomes salvation at the end of Van Helsing's stake and 'dies' with a contented smile. It's a theme carried from the original novel through Fisher's entire oeuvre, one as blatant as the penetration motif of the vampire myth.

Vadim, on the other hand, breaks with tradition. Mircalla's vampire dismisses such Puritanism and actually has the audacity to win. Unlike her hissing namesakes in **Brides**, she triumphs (making evil victorious for one of the first times in contemporary cinema).

It's easy to see why **Blood and Roses** suffered at the hands of the censors while Fisher's picture, despite some subversive flourishes, passed largely unscathed. Its very controversy rendered Vadim's work the more influential, forming the template for subsequent British vampires, particularly Hammer's own line of Carmilla exploitations (**The Vampire Lovers**, **Lust for a Vampire**, and **Twins of Evil**).

Beyond that, it freed vampire cinema from its historic conventions. By setting **Blood and Roses** in contemporary Italy, Roger Vadim spearheaded a new kind of Gothic cinema, one of lasting resonance (from Harry Kümel's **La rouge aux lèvres** (aka **Daughters of Darkness**, 1971) to José Larraz's **Vampyres** (1974).

Nowhere is this influence more apparent than in the work of French auteur Jean Rollin. Beginning with **Le viol du vampire** (aka **The Rape of the Vampire**, 1968) through his later work, such as **La fiancée de Dracula** (2002), Rollin instilled his films with the same themes, sexuality and picture-postcard composition. His female vampires, distillations of Stroyberg's Carmilla, prowl fairytale landscapes in diaphanous gowns, pushing the homoerotic aspects to their limit.

By comparison, **Blood and Roses** seems a rather restrained affair. Its languid pace, in fact, has inspired more than one contemporary critic to label it 'slow moving'.

Expecting a terror juggernaut of the film invites disappointment. Like the first half-hour of **The Brides of Dracula**, before Van Helsing's appearance and Errol Flynn theatrics, **Blood and Roses** is an adult fantasy with a nod to the romantic. (It's worth noting that the same critique was levelled against Fisher's criminally underrated **The Phantom of the Opera**, nearly costing the director his career.)

Open-eyed examination of **Blood and Roses** reveals a film of surprising complexity. Indeed, if imitation can be considered the sincerest form of flattery, Stroyberg's passive reading – disembodied, possessed – can be seen as quintessential. It was to become the hallmark of the female succubus, informing not only Hammer and Jean Rollin's work, but entire generations of bloodsuckers, witches and ghouls. It also allowed the female vampire to escape the shadow of Dracula's domineering male sexuality and opened interpretation beyond the British class system debate (by which Dracula was bound to the antiquated aristocracy).

Much has been made, of course, of Vadim's attempts to objectify his spouses at the cost of his art – a process begun with Brigitte Bardot in **…And God Created Woman** (1956) and reinforced by his self-serving autobiography *Bardot, Deneuve, Fonda: My Life with the Three Most Beautiful Women in the World* (1988). It's a tribute to Stroyberg that her performance has withstood the test of time. Whatever Vadim's motivation, exploitation or objectification, she remains an influential presence.

The other principals, while hardly as absorbing, handle their roles with gusto. Mel Ferrer, fresh from an appearance with Christopher Lee in **The Hands of Orlac** (1960), makes a fine romantic foil (compare his scenery chewing in Tobe Hooper's **Eaten Alive** (aka **Death Trap**, 1976) for a healthy laugh).

above: The lauded costume party sequence in **Blood and Roses**.
below: Roger Vadim and his wife Annette, working together on the film.

It's the beautiful Elsa Martinelli who offers Stroyberg her only real competition, finely balancing innocence with sexual awakening. It's a pity that she was never again offered a part with such potential, despite brushes with John Wayne (1962's **Hatari!**) and Ursula Andress (1965's **La decima vittima** aka **The Tenth Victim**).

The trump card for **Blood and Roses**, however, comes in the form of its artisans. At their forefront stands Jean Prodromidés, who offers a stately score that draws inspiration from the classics, combining earthy strings and lilting harp. The main theme, which punctuates both the film's opening and closing monologues, is every bit as haunting as the images.

Not to be upstaged, legendary cinematographer Claude Renoir imbues the images with a life of their own (note his masterful introduction of the film's characters, as the frame glides about the room, caressing each in turn). Never sacrificing composition – in fact, creating it effortlessly – he crafts images of sheer magnificence. Apprenticing as a camera operator for his uncle, Jean Renoir – on no less than **Le grande illusion** (1937) – Claude had become world-renowned by the time of **Blood and Roses**. His association with Vadim would continue for a number of fantasy projects, with the Italian omnibus **Histoires extraordinaires** (aka **Spirits of the Dead**, 1967) and widely-heralded **Barbarella** (1968), both using his eye to keen effect.

These collaborations also served to demonstrate the magic of this teaming. Neither man, despite substantial budget increases, would ever recapture the delirious intensity of these films. Vadim's post-sixties work began to border on self-parody (witness 1988's tepid remake **And God Created Woman**), while Renoir found himself tied to unimaginative directors (e.g. 1977's woeful **The Spy Who Loved Me**, a box-office smash despite its listlessness).

this page: A variety of images from Roger Vadim's **Blood and Roses** that demonstrate the film's heady mix of elegance, beauty, surrealism, menace and drama. Unfairly overlooked in most appraisals of vampire film history, this film is ripe for rediscovery.

To dissect **Blood and Roses** is to find both men at the height of their powers: There's the revelation of Mircalla's crypt, a symphony of fog and crosses climaxed by Stroyberg's caress of a stone effigy (which accesses the vampire's body in perfect dream logic).

There's the celebrated costume party encounter between Ferrer, in quintessential bat mask, and Martinelli. As the lovers enjoy a playful embrace, the camera suddenly rises over a concealing hedge, revealing the scope of the party beyond (and reintroducing the real world).

There's the fox hunt, the girls arranged like Monet subjects beneath arching trees, Carmilla overcome by the offer of Georgia's throat while the men conduct their bloody ritual around them.

Which is not to say that **Blood and Roses** is an unqualified masterpiece. There are several moments of painful comic relief, notably a musical exchange between Carmilla and Leopoldo, that are enough to make audiences cringe.

It's tempting to dismiss these as antiquated intrusions, holdovers from the heyday of Universal, when it was believed that audiences were incapable of sustained terror without comic respites. Certainly, they are common to the work of both Hammer and Terence Fisher, who typically appointed an alcoholic priest or doctor to the task.

Nevertheless, **Blood and Roses** triumphs despite such lamentable intrusions, a milestone of both vampire and erotic cinema.

BFI FLIPSIDE

discover film

"Flipside is not just a dynamite DVD label, but a goldmine of great British Cinema."

Nicolas Winding Refn, director of *Bronson* and *Valhalla Rising*

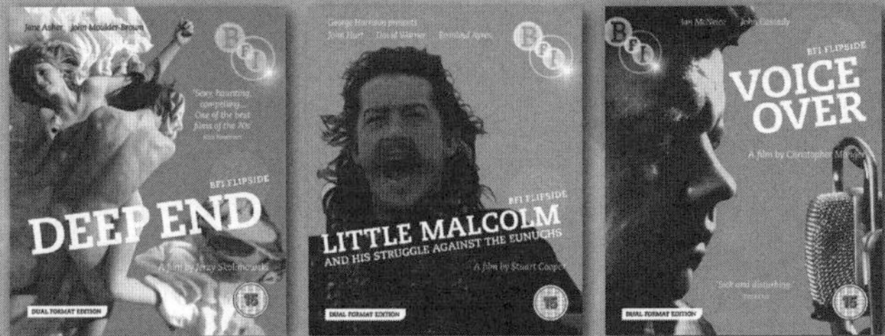

Coming soon from the Flipside:

- The chillingly dark comedy *Little Malcolm* starring John Hurt, directed by Stuart Cooper (*Overlord*) and financed by George Harrison.

- The disturbing drama *Voice Over* which stars Ian McNeice and has remained unseen since its controversial cinema release in 1983.

Order now from **amazon**.co.uk

Page references in **bold** refer exclusively to illustrations, though pages referenced as text may also features relevant illustrations.

7th Commandment, The 68
28 Days Later 22
1941 22
2001: A Space Odyssey 57
Adams, Phillip 57
Addams Family, The (TV series) 81
Addams, Dawn 10, 11
Africa addio 52
Africa ama 52
Africa, Blood and Guts see Africa addio
Airplane! 64
Aleksic, Dragoljub 27
Alfaro, Italo 50
Alfred the Great 8
Allen, Nancy 74
American Graffiti 20
American History X 60
American Pie 20
American Werewolf in London, An 20, 21, 23
And God Created Woman (1956) 91
And God Created Woman (1988) 92
Andress, Ursula 91
Angels from Hell 11
Antonioni, Michelangelo 43, 73
Apocalypse Now 39
arcidiavolo, L' 47
Aretino, Pietro 41, 49
Arkoff, Samuel Z. 7
armata Brancaleone, L' 41, 47
Army of Darkness 82, **87**
Attack of the Helping Hand (short) 81
Avengers, The (TV series) 15
Aykroyd, Dan 22, 23, 25
Baby of Mâcon, The 71
Bad Taste 82, 85, **87**
Baker, Rick 20
Baker, Roy Ward 8, 11
Barbarella 7, 92
Bardot, Brigitte 91
Barry Lyndon 57
Basic Instinct 78-79
Basket Case 82, **87**
Bastedo, Alexandra 18
Bates, Ralph 13
Bawdy Tales see Storie scellerate
Beast with Five Fingers, The 81
Beffe, licenze et amori del Decamerone segreto 45, 53
bella Antonia, prima Monica e poi dimonia, La 49-50
Belushi, John 20, 22, 23, 25
Belzberg, Leslie 23
Beolco, Angelo 41, 47
Beresford, Bruce 57
Bergin, Thomas 42, 43, 53
Berkley, Elizabeth **76**
Bernardi, Massimo 52
betia, ovvero in amore per ogni gaudenza ci vuole sofferenza, La 41, 47
Betts, Kirsten see Lindholm, Kirsten
Beverly Hills Cop 25
Beverly Hills Cop III 25
Beyond Re-Animator 82
Bianchini, Paolo 48
Bibbiena, Cardinal 41
Birkinshaw, Alan 35-39
Black Book 72, **77**
Black Decameron, The see Decamerone nero, Il
Black, Isobel 11, 18
Blood and Roses 7, 89-92
Blood of Fu Manchu, The 8
Blood Spattered Bride, The 18
Blues Brothers, The 20, 22-23
Blues Brothers 2000 23
Blues Traveler 23
Blumenstock, Peter 14
Boccaccio '70 41, **42**
Boccaccio, Giovanni 41-43, 45-54
Bordigoni, Sandra 58
Bouchet, Barbara 48
Brain That Wouldn't Die, The 70
Braindead **80**, 82, 85, 86, **87**
Brancaleone alle Crociate 41, **43**, 47
Brancaleone at the Crusades see Brancaleone alle Crociate
Brazil 71
Brest, Martin 25
Bride of Re-Animator 82
Brides of Dracula, The 12, 14, 90, 91
Brown, Clancy **75**
Brown, James 23
Bunussi, Femi 48
Bush, Dick 17
Butch Cassidy and the Sundance Kid 14
Cabinet of Dr. Caligari, The 7
Calloway, Cab 23

Campanile, Pasquale Festa 46, 47
Campbell, Bruce 81, 82, **87**
Can You Keep It Up for a Week? 14
Canterbury proibito **54**
Canterbury Tales, The (book) 42
Caponi, Aldo 48
Captain Clegg 10
Captain Kronos: Vampire Hunter 18
Carmilla (novella) 7, 89
Carreras, James 7, 8, 10, 12-15
Carreras, Michael 18
cavalla tutta nuda, Una 48
Chaplin, Charlie 82, 83, 88
Charles, Ray 23
Chastity Belt, The see cintura di castità, La
Chaucer, Geoffrey 41, 42
Cherry Falls 57, 63-64
Chomsky, Noam 74
cintura di castità, La 47
Citti, Franco 46
Citti, Sergio 46
Clapton, Eric 23
Clark, Christoph 54
Clemens, Brian 18
Clémenti, Pierre **26**, **28**, 29
Clockwork Orange, A 57
Club, The 57
Cocteau, Jean 90
Cole, George 10, 11
Collins, Joan 7
Collinson, Madeleine 15-17
Collinson, Mary 15-17
Comedy Without a Title (book) 47
Coming to America 23, 25
Confessions of a Sex Maniac 35-36
Confessions of a Window Cleaner 14
Conspirators of Pleasure 71
Contraband see Luca il contrabbandiere
Crescendo 8, 10
Crostarosa, Dado 48
Crowe, Russell **56**, 58, 59, 61
Crypt of Horror 7
Cushing, Peter 8, 11-14, 16-18
Dale, Alan 82, 83
Damaged Goods 67
D'Amato, Joe see Massaccesi, Aristide
Damiano, Luca 52, 54
Dance of the Vampires 11
Dandolo, Lucio 41, 48
Daughters of Darkness 18
Daughters of Darkness see rouge aux lèvres, La
Davoli, Ninetto 46
Dawn of the Dead (1978) 81, 82
Dawn of the Dead (2004) 22
De Bosio, Gianfranco 41, 47
De Laurentiis, Dino 19, 20
De Martino, Alberto 54
De Santis, Orchidea 48
De Sica, Vittorio 41
Death Trap see Eaten Alive
Decameron, The 41, 44-46, 48, 50
Decameron, The (book) 41-47, 49-54
Decameron No. 2 - Le altre novelle del Boccaccio 48-50
Decameron No. 3 - Le più belle donne del Boccaccio 50, **51**
Decameron No. 4 - Le belle novelle del Boccaccio 48
Decamerone nero, Il 52, 53
Deer Woman (TV episode) 21
Delfont, Bernard 12, 14
Deodato, Ruggero 47
Devil in Love, The see arcidiavolo, L'
Devil Rides Out, The 17
Diddley, Bo 23
Doctor Detroit 25
Doctor in the House 8
Doctor in Trouble 13
Donovan's Brain 70
Douglas, Michael 78
Dr. Strangelove 57
Dracula (1931) 7
Dracula (1958) 90
Dracula (novel) 7, 89
Dracula Has Risen from the Grave 13
Dravic, Milena 28
Dreyer, Carl 7
Dunne, Griffin **21**
Dyall, Valentine 13
Eaten Alive 91
Eaton, Shirley 8, 11
Ebert, Roger 22, 32
Edmond 19
Egyptian, The 39
Eraserhead 71
Esper, Dwain 67-71

Esposito, Riccardo 50
Evil Dead 2: Dead By Dawn 81, 82, 84, 85, **87**
Evil Dead, The 82, 84, 87
Eyes Without a Face see yeux sans visage, Les
Fanfani, Amintore 43
Farewell to Arms, A (book) 81
Fellini, Federico 41, 43, 53
Fenech, Edwige 49, 50
Ferrer, Mel 89, 91, 92
fiancée de Dracula, La 91
Fields, W.C. 81
Finch, Jon **6**, 11
Fine, Harry 7, 8, 10, 12, 14, 15
Fine, Larry **80**, **84**
Fisher, Terence 12, 14, 90-92
For Love and Gold see armata Brancaleone, L'
Forbidden Decameron **40**
Four Days of Naples, The see quattro giornate di Napoli, Le
Fourth Man, The 74, 79
Fra'Tazio da Velletri 41
Franju, Georges 90
Frankenstein 69
Franklin, Aretha 23
Fratello homo sorella bona - nel Boccaccio superproibito 53
Fréjaville, Gustave 82
Frenzy 11
Frey, Sami 30
Friedman, David F. 68
Fulci, Lucio 46
Gailey, Lynn 58
Gale, David 85
Garris, Mick 25
Gassman, Vittorio **43**, **47**
Gastaldi, Romano 41
Gates, Tudor 7, 8, 11-16, 18
Gaunt, Valerie 11
Gemser, Laura 35
Gilliam, Terry 71
Ginsborg, Paul 44
Giordano, Marlangela 48
Giorgelli, Gabriella 48
Giotto 45, 46
Godwin, Frank 14
Godzilla 19
Goldfinger 8
Goldwyn, Sam 21
Gomarasca, Manlio 41, 54
Good, JoAnne **34**
Goodman, John 23
Gordon, Stuart 19-23, 84
grande illusion, La 92
Green Hornet, The (TV series) 19
Greenaway, Peter 71
Greenberg, Bob 20, 21
Greene, Naomi 44
Guerrasio, Guido 52
Guerrini, Mino 48-50
Hall, Harvey 13, 16
Hands of Orlac, The 91
Hands of the Ripper 16, 17
Harbou, Thea von 67
Hardy, Oliver 82, 84, 86
Harryhausen, Ray 19
Haunted House of Horror, The 8
Hemingway, Ernest 81
Henenlotter, Frank 82
Henry: Portrait of a Serial Killer 85
Heyward, 'Deke' 8
Highway to Hell 67
Hitchcock, Alfred 11, 73
Hitler, Adolf 58, 60, 61, 77
Hollow Man 75
Holmes, John 42
Holocaust Industry, The (book) 77
Honey, I Shrunk the Kids 22
Hooker, John Lee 23
Hooper, Tobe 91
Horror of Frankenstein 12, 13
Hough, John 15, 16, 18
Howard, Curly **80**, **84**
Howard, Moe **80**, **84**
Hughes, William 14
Hunger, The 18
I Married a Savage 67
In Love, Every Pleasure Has Its Pain see betia, ovvero in amore per ogni gaudenza ci vuole sofferenza, La
Innocence Unprotected 27
Innocent Blood **24**, 25
Invaders of the Lost Gold 35, 38-39
Jackson, Peter 82, 84, 85, **87**
Jacopetti, Gualtiero 52, 53
Jones, Gillian 57

Jordan, Michael 19
Journey to Old Yugoslavia, The (short) 27
Keaton, Buster 82, 85, 88
Keaton, Camille 48, 49
Keep It Up Downstairs 14
Keil, Margaret Rose 48
Kentucky Fried Movie, The 19, 20
Kerekes, David 52
Kershaw, Ian 77
Kessler, Christian 54
Killer's Moon 34, 35-36, 38, **39**
Killing for Culture (book) 52
Kim, Evan 19
King Kong 19
Kracauer, Siegfried 83, 87, 88
Kubrick, Stanley 57
Kümel, Harry 91
Lair of the White Worm, The 71
Landis, John 19-25
Landis, Max 21
Lang, Fritz 67, 73
Larraz, José 91
Last Decameron: Adultery in 7 Easy Lessons, The see Decameron
No. 3 - Le più belle donne del Boccaccio
Last Man on Earth, The 22
Laure, Carole 29, 30, **31**, 32, **33**
Laurenti, Mariano 49, 50, 53
Lawrence, Brian 8
Le Fanu, Joseph Sheridan 7, 11, 18, 89
Lee, Bruce 19
Lee, Christopher 7, 8, 13, 16, 91
Leigh, Suzanna 7, 13
Lenzi, Umberto 46
Lester, Richard 20
Lewis, Jerry 25
Lindholm, Kirsten **1**, 10, **12**, 13, 16, 18
Lipson, Frank 63
Lloyd, Harold 82
LoDuca, Joseph 81, 84
Loggia, Robert 25
Longhurst, Sue 13
Longo, Malisa 48, **50**, 53
Lord of the Rings, The 85
Losers, The 14
Love Affair, or the Case of the Missing Switchboard Operator 27
Love Boccaccio Style 42, 53
Loverboy 57, 58
Luca il contrabbandiere 46
Lust for a Vampire 11-14, 18, 90
Lusty Wives of Canterbury, The 48
Lynch, David 71
Macbeth 11
Macy, William H. 21
Maddin, Guy 71
Makavejev, Dusan 27-32
Man Is Not a Bird 27
Maniac **66**, 67-71
Mantegna, Joe 21
Marcabru 50
Marihuana 67-69
Martell, Philip 14
Martin, Dean 25
Martin, Steve 22
Martinelli, Elsa 89, 91, 92
Martines, Lauro 45
Massacesi, Aristide 52-54
Masters of Horror (TV series) 21
Matheson, Judy 13, 18
Matheson, Richard Christian 25
Mayne, Ferdy 11
McKenzie, Jacqueline 61
Medea 44
Mendelsohn, Ben 57
Metal Skin 57, 58, 62-63, **65**
Michelle, Ann 15
Michelle, Vicki 15
Miles, Margaret 45
Million Eyes of Sumuru, The 8
Modern Motherhood 67, 68
Modern Times 83
Mondo cane 52
Monicelli, Mario 41, 47
Monique 7
Monlaur, Yvonne 90
Moon Zero Two 12
Moore, Irving 17
More Sexy Canterbury Tales see Sollazzevoli storie di mogli
gaudenti e mariti penitenti - Decameron nº 69
Morin, Edgar 43
Moro, Aldo 44
Morris, Aubrey 8
Mulisch, Harry 77
Mummy's Shroud, The 12
Munro, Caroline 15
Murphy, Brittany **64**
Murphy, Eddie 25

Mystery of Birth 67
Napoli violenta 46
Narcotic **66**, 67-69
National Lampoon's Animal House 20, 23, 25
Natural Born Killers 59
Naughty in New Orleans 67
Naughty Nun see bella Antonia, prima Monica e poi dimonia, La
Nell, Krista 48
Nichols, Mike 20
Nicholson, James H. 7
Nicolai, Bruno 50
Night of the Living Dead 22
No Greater Sin 67
Novelle licenziose di vergini vogliose 52
Nudist Recruits 67
Oi! Warning 60
O'Mara, Kate 10, 11, 15
Ophuls, Max 73
Orpheus 90
Parillaud, Anne **24**, **25**
Pasolini, Pier Paolo 32, 41, 43-50, 52, 54
Paths of Glory 57
Peters, Luan 18
Phantom of the Opera, The 91
Phillips, Sam 41, 42, 53
Pinches, George 8
Pitsi 27
Pitt, Ingrid **6**, 8, **9**, 10-13, 18
Pleasure Girls, The 7
Poe, Edgar Allan 69, 71
Polanski, Roman 11, 38
Pollock, Daniel 57, 61
Preston, Billy 23
Price, Vincent 22
Primitive Passion 67
Prior, Richard 25
Prodromidès, Jean 92
Prosperi, Franco 52, 53
Prucnal, Anna **26**, **28**, 29, 31
Pulici, Davide 52
Purdom, Edmond 35, 39
Quant'è bella la Bernarda, tutta nera, tutta calda 41
Quarry, Robert 18
quattro giornate di Napoli, Le 46
Quel gran pezzo della Ubalda tutta nuda e tutta calda 49, 50,
51, 53
Ragionamenti (book) 49
Raimi, Sam 81, 84, 85, 87, 88
Rambaldi, Carlo 19
Rape of the Vampire, The see viol du vampire, Le
Raven, Mike 13
Re-Animator 20-22, 69, 82, 85, 86
Redway, John 8
Reefer Madness 67, 69
Regoli, Maria Piera 52
Reich, Wilhelm 27
Renoir, Claude 92
Renoir, Jean 92
Return of Count Yorga, The 18
Ribald Decameron, The see Beffe, licenze et amori del Decamerone
segreto
Richmond, Anthony 57
Rickles, Don 25
Riefenstahl, Leni 75
Rio 70 8
Robertson, Harry 14, 18
Robinson, Brian 57
RoboCop 74
Rohmer, Sax 8
Rollin, Jean 91
Roman Scandals '73 see Fratello homo sorella bona - nel
Boccaccio superproibito
Romero, George A. 21, 22, 81
Romper Stomper **56**, 57-63
Rossetti, Franco 48
rouge aux lèvres, La 91
Russell, Ken 71
Sacchetti, Franco 42
Saint, The (TV series) 15
Sakata, Harold 35
Sangster, Jimmy 12-15
Scansati... a Trinità arriva Eldorado 52
Scars of Dracula 8, 14
Scary Movie 64
Scharf, Daniel 58
Scola, Ettore 47
Scream and Scream Again 7
Secret Africa 52
Sequi, Mario 53
Shelley, Mary 69
Shine 57
Showgirls **76**
Sinister Menace 69
Sirk, Douglas 73
Skeggs, Roy 12

Slapstick! The Illustrated Story of Knockabout Comedy (book) 82
Slater, David 52
Smith, Madeline **6**, 10, 11
Snow White and the Seven Dwarfs 27
Sollazzevoli storie di mogli gaudenti e mariti penitenti -
Decameron nº 69 52
Sopranos, The (TV series) 25
Spataro, Diego 52
Spider-Man 85
Spider-Man 3 23
Spiegel, Scott 81
Spies Like Us 20
Spirits of the Dead see Histoires extraordinaires
Spomenicima Ne Treba Verovati (short) 27
Spy Who Loved Me, The 19, 92
Stadie, Hildegarde 67, 69
Starship Troopers 74, 75, 77
Staveacre, Tony 82
Stay Away from Trinity... When He Comes to Eldorado see
Scansati... a Trinità arriva Eldorado
Steel, Pippa 11, 13
Stensgaard, Yutte 12, 14
Stoker, Bram 7, 89, 90
Stone, Sharon 78, 79
Storie scellerate 46
Straight On Till Morning 16
Stroyberg, Annette 89, 91, 92
Style, Michael 7, 10, 14, 15
Subterfuge 7, 13
Surviving Eden **19**
Svankmajer, Jan 71
Sweet Movie **26**, 27-32, **33**
Tannahill, Reay 48
Taste the Blood of Dracula 10
Taylor, Frederick 83
Taylor, Noah 57
Ten Little Indians 8
Tenser, Tony 7
Thomas, Damien 16, **18**
Thorson, Linda 15
Three Amigos! 23
Trading Places 23, 25
Trecento novelle (book) 42
Trevelyan, John 10
Triumph of the Will 77
Truffaut, François 73
Twins of Evil 15-18, 90
Two Faces of Dr. Jekyll, The 10
Ubalda, All Naked and Warm see Quel gran pezzo della Ubalda
tutta nuda e tutta calda
Vadim, Roger 7, 89-92
Vailland, Roger 89
Vamp 18
Vampire Lovers, The **1**, **6**, 7-8, **9**, 10-12, 14, 18, 90
Vampyr 7
Vampyres 18, 91
Vari, Giuseppe 53
Velvet Vampire, The 18
vergine per il principe, Una 47
Verhoeven, Paul 73-79
Vernon, John 29
viol du vampire, Le 91
Violent Naples see Napoli violenta
Virgin for the Prince, A see vergine per il principe, Una
Virgin Witch 15
Visconti, Luchino 41, 53
Vivarelli, Piero 52, 53
Walter, Little 23
Washington Jr., Grover 23
Wasserman, John L. 11
Wayne, John 91
Weldon, Fay 36
Weller, Peter 74
Wells, Junior 23
Wertmuller, Lina 73
When Dinosaurs Ruled the Earth 12
Where Eagles Dare 8
Whitman, Stuart 35, 38, 39
Wilder, Billy 73
Wilder, Gene 25
Wilmer, Douglas **8**, 11
Witty Stories of Whoring Wives and Cuckolded Husbands 54
Wolfshead: The Legend of Robin Hood 15
Wood, Bret 68, 70
Wood, Ed 68
WR: Mysteries of the Organism 27-28
Wright, Geoffrey 57-64
Wright, Maggie 18
Wyeth, Katya 16-18
Wyler, William 21
yeux sans visage, Les 90
Young, Aden **62**, **65**
Yuzna, Brian 20-22
Zenabel 47
Zeta One 13

More Essential Cinema Books from FAB Press

Beasts in the Cellar
Exploitation Film Career of Tony Tenser

ISBN 978-1-903254-27-1
UK £17.99 / US $29.95

304pp. 272mm x 192mm

Any Gun Can Play
The Essential Guide to Euro-Westerns

ISBN 978-1-903254-61-5
UK £24.99 / US $39.95

480pp. 254mm x 192mm

Agitator
The cinema of Takashi Miike

ISBN 978-1-903254-41-7
UK £17.99 / US $29.95

432pp. 244mm x 171mm

Behind the Pink Curtain
Complete History of Japanese Sex Cinema

ISBN 978-1-903254-54-7
UK £19.99 / US $34.95

416pp. 254mm x 192mm

Blaxploitation Cinema
The Essential Reference Guide

ISBN 978-1-903254-44-8
UK £15.99 / US $27.95

240pp. 254mm x 192mm

Cinema Sewer
Volume Three

ISBN 978-1-903254-64-6
UK £12.99 / US $19.95

192pp. 244mm x 171mm

Iron Man
The cinema of Shinya Tsukamoto

ISBN 978-1-903254-36-3
UK £14.99 / US $24.95

240pp. 244mm x 171mm

The Art of
the Nasty

ISBN 978-1-903254-57-8
UK £19.99 / US $34.95

168pp. 295mm x 221mm

Cannibal Holocaust
Savage Cinema of Ruggero Deodato

ISBN 978-1-903254-65-3
UK £19.99 / US $34.95

128pp. 303mm x 213mm

For further information about these books, and more from the FAB Press range, please visit our
online store, where we also carry a fine selection of up to date horror film magazines.

www.fabpress.com